A Treasury of the Cross

By the same author

❧ ❦

CHURCH PAGEANTRY

RELIGIOUS DRAMAS

NEW TESTAMENT WOMEN AND PROBLEMS OF TODAY

THE MERCHANT OF THE MÛRISTÂN

FOOTPRINTS IN PALESTINE

MY HOBBY OF THE CROSS

THE JOURNEY OF THE CHRIST CHILD

Co-author with J. Lane Miller

CRUISING THE MEDITERRANEAN

AN ENCYCLOPEDIA OF BIBLE LIFE

HARPER'S BIBLE DICTIONARY

A Treasury of the Cross

MADELEINE S. MILLER

(MRS. J. LANE MILLER)

Photographs by J. Lane Miller

Drawings by Claire Valentine

Harper & Brothers Publishers, New York

Special acknowledgment is made to the following, who have granted permission for the reprinting of copyrighted material from the books, periodicals, monographs, and newspapers listed below; or for the use of poems and other material whose copyright they control:

ABINGDON PRESS: *The Beginning of Christianity* by Clarence Tucker Craig, copyright, 1943, by Whitmore & Stone; *In the Light of the Cross* by Harold Cooke Phillips, copyright, 1947, by Stone & Pierce; *An Introduction to New Testament Thought* by Frederick C. Grant, copyright, 1950, by Pierce & Smith; *Prayer* by George Arthur Buttrick, copyright, 1942, by Whitmore & Stone; *The Early Church and the Coming Great Church* by John Knox, copyright, 1955, by Pierce & Washabaugh.

WALTER H. BAKER CO.: "God's Way" from *Twelve Months of Drama for the Average Church* by Dorothy Clarke Wilson, copyright, 1933, by Walter H. Baker Co. (also permission of the author).

BRANDT & BRANDT: sonnet from *Mine the Harvest* by Edna St. Vincent Millay, copyright, 1952, by Norma Millay Ellis.

MRS. THOMAS CURTIS CLARK: "The Cross upon a Hill" by Thomas Curtis Clark.

CLARKE & STUART CO., LTD., Vancouver: "Crucifixion" by Frederick George Scott, copyright, 1934, by Clarke & Stuart Co., Ltd.

CHRISTIAN ADVOCATE: material in articles by Madeleine S. Miller, April 13, 1933, and March 29, 1934. Copyright, 1933, 1934, by Christian Advocate.

CHRISTIAN HERALD: "To-day . . . Paradise" by Madeleine S. Miller, copyright, 1954, by Christian Herald, Inc.; part of article "Don't Be Afraid of Tomorrow" by Madeleine S. Miller, copyright, March 1954, by Christian Herald, Inc.

MRS. HARRY WEBB FARRINGTON: selection from "Our Christ" by Harry Webb Farrington.

FREDERICK C. GRANT (see The Macmillan Company).

In Dulcem Memoriam

―――――◆―――――

J. LANE MILLER

my "good minister of Christ Jesus," who has
sponsored and encouraged me in the finding and
evaluating of crosses of Christendom in lands we
have traveled together, and has helped me carry
my own heaviest cross

CONTENTS

*Drawings will be found
on pages 55–60*

*Illustrations will be found
following page 80*

ACKNOWLEDGMENTS

The most pleasant part of writing a book is the expression of appreciation to those who have given assistance. The toil and heat of developing the chapters are behind. There remains only the privilege of thanking the gracious persons who have shared their works and their wisdom and have offered answers to baffling questions.

The following scholars have enriched our information: Dr. Homer A. Thompson, whose name will long be linked with the excavation of the Agora at Athens by the American School of Classical Studies; Professor Amadeo Maiuri, Director of Archaeological Investigations in the Campania, Italy; Dr. Schuyler Van R. Cammann of the Museum of the University of Pennsylvania; Dr. John S. Thatcher, Director of the Dumbarton Oaks Research Library and Collection of Harvard University; Rosalie B. Green, Director of the Index of Christian Art at Princeton University. Appreciation is expressed for information supplied by Harriett Seibert, Marion Derby, Marie Louise Riall; F. A. Nixon, whose studies of Nestorian crosses have been informative.

The reference departments of libraries have been generous in supplying information: the library of Union Theological Seminary, whose reference librarian, Mrs. Hugh M. Foster, has been gracious in encouragement and advice; the Zion

Research Library of Brookline, Massachusetts, whose A. Marguerite Smith—my Vassar classmate—has for years been generous; the library of Pittsburgh-Xenia Theological Seminary, Pittsburgh, Pennsylvania, whose librarian, Agnes L. Valentine, has helped me feel at home again in my home city; and especially the Carnegie Library of Pittsburgh, whose large staff of expert reference librarians has been tireless in helping locate essential information.

Several poets have permitted free quotation of their own work, as indicated on the copyright page. Particular appreciation is extended to Miss Erica Oxenham, daughter of the British poet John Oxenham, for allowing the use of a number of lines from her father's poems. The Rev. Thomas Tiplady of London has generously allowed the inclusion of his great hymn, "Above the Hills of Time."

To Canon Edward N. West of the Cathedral of St. John the Divine in New York is expressed appreciation for his reading of the entire manuscript and for valuable suggestions; also for granting permission to quote from his own *Meditations on the Gospel of St. John.* Canon Charles T. Bridgeman, formerly of St. George's Cathedal, Jerusalem, has supplied historical data pertaining to the ancient churches of the Near East. The Near East Society and the Near East Magazine have supplied data concerning lands of the cross; and the Greek Archdiocese of North and South America has made available material pertaining to the Greek Orthodox Church.

Ira W. Martin is thanked for some of the photographs.

The Fleming H. Revell Company has kindly granted permission for the incorporation of portions of *My Hobby of the*

Cross, including the use of some of the plates of illustrations.

The author expresses warm appreciation of the patient editorial assistance rendered by Eleanor Jordan of Harper & Brothers.

The reader is invited to search for his own symbols of Christian faith. Yet in a sense he cannot seek his crosses. *They must find him.* But by his reaction to them, he will discover the quality of his own Christian fortitude.

MADELEINE S. MILLER

(MRS. J. LANE MILLER)

Pittsburgh, Pennsylvania
April 30, 1956

PART I

❧

Our First Crosses

IT ALL began unexpectedly on a happy afternoon between two world wars. While sauntering on the Athenian Acropolis, that glowing hilltop of world history and religious art, my husband and I were overtaken by an American archaeologist. He had been observing Lane's interest in fragments of Greek pottery lying on the ground among bits of Pentelic marble chipped off Parthenon columns during current restoration by American Friends of Greece.

"If you like eloquent Greek fragments," the scholar suggested to my husband, "why don't you buy an intact vase or two? There is a fascinating old bazaar where such things are found."

"It is too easy to be duped in the matter of ancient potsherds," Lane replied. "Dealers make vases one day, crack them up with a hammer the next, and on the third, put them together so cleverly that they soon sell for authentic antiques."

The professor laughed. "If you will trust my judgment," he said, "I will lead you to a reliable shop. Few travelers stumble upon it. It is just off Shoe Lane, down near St. Irene's."

So, without dreaming that we were on the eve of being discovered by what became a permanent interest during more than 100,000 miles of travel and years of subsequent study, we followed the professor, picking our way down the steep steps from the Acropolis, along the Boulevard of St. Paul, on past the Theater of Dionysus, where Athenians twenty thousand strong once jammed the seats and surrounding hillsides for performances of *Electra* and *Agamemnon*. But we were headed for the bazaars.

The Athens bazaar to which our archaeologist friend led us is at the head of Pandrossou Street which intersects Aeolus Street, leading appropriately north from the octagonal first-century Tower of the Winds with its noted water clock. Turning a sudden corner on Shoe Lane, we found ourselves in a paved alley of small antique shops, each worth lingering in.

Arriving at the proper shop, the archaeologist and Lane examined slender clay vases such as those which, in the fifth century B.C., built up the prosperity as well as the art reputation of Athens. There were amphorae, once used as prizes in Athenian games; black and red Corinthian primitives; Mycenaean ware; and fifth-century hydria with natural red clay figures on black-painted backgrounds. Just as Lane and the shop owner were closing a deal for an eight-inch graceful Tanagra rose-red oil vase decorated with black horses and helmeted warriors of twenty-five hundred years ago, my eye lighted on a velvet tray of jumbled jewelry. At first glance most of it appeared dusty trash—but how precious some of it became to us later.

The piece which attracted me most was a cross of faded gold filigree, studded with red and blue cabochons, or stones, suggesting the taste of Byzantine Christians in Justinian's sixth-century Constantinople. It had come from the island of Crete, home of prehistoric art two thousand years before the Christian Era. Although this cross in Pandrossou Street dated only two hundred years back, its design bore the ancient elegance of Crete. From both arms hung tiny pendant crosses of pierced gold. Above its head was a filigree canopy topped with a crown of petals, as of a passion flower. This Cretan cross pleaded with me to possess it. Beauty and eloquent symbolic meaning shone from its chaste design.

"We'll take this fine Cretan cross," announced my husband to the antiquarian, without asking the price. Fortunately Mr. Philip, the shopkeeper, was an honest man and asked only three American dollars in exchange for the cross, which became the pioneer member of our collection. Our interest whetted, we looked at other items on the tray and found a still older square silver amulet on which was a crudely scratched cross. Its crooked edges and its hand-rubbed silver, in places worn into holes, spoke of reverent craftsmanship and long use. On one side was embossed a square Greek cross and on the reverse, a gallant St. George on his horse, attacking the traditional Mediterranean dragon who was said to torture guileless maidens. In the Mediterranean area we were to meet this popular hero again in the St. George murals in the fifteenth-century Church of San Giorgio degli Schiavoni in Venice; again in Beirut, whose modern Hotel St. George carries on its baggage labels reminders of the saint's knightly exploits.

The legend of St. George and the virtuous princess whom

he rescued from the fiery dragon near Silene in Lybia spread early throughout the Middle East, possibly having sprung from the tale of the Iranian deity, Verethragna. The legends were adapted to the culture of the seventh and eighth centuries and of course were Christianized and embellished by Crusaders on their Eastern campaigns of pious warfare. At Cyprus, the festival of St. George is celebrated on April 23, when the sick are brought out to be cured. At Larnaca children late in walking are carried to the Monastery of St. George at the time of the new moon. And in other parts of the island, girls late in finding husbands are promised hope if they knock at the door of St. George's Church, saying, "So may the bridegroom knock at our home."

When we left Mr. Philip's shop the St. George amulet accompanied us. I have never worn the first cross we purchased that day but for years I have fingered the smooth old silver box and its square Greek cross and have wondered what reverent craftsman in what silver-foamed Aegean island fashioned it, and when and for whom.

One evening a year or so later, we were looking through our cabinet of crosses in the parsonage living room. Upon examining again the old St. George amulet we drew out the slim little slide which forms the lid to this venerable box. There was disclosed a puzzling feature—something appeared to be concealed within it. With a pin we dislodged from inside the amulet a tiny fragment of disintegrating cloth, a morsel of worm-eaten wood, and a segment of old coin. Evidently some credulous Greek peasant had thought them to be holy relics, probably obtaining them in exchange for aprons or jackets heavily ornamented with colorful hand embroidery requiring months of winter work. No doubt some itinerant peddler had foisted upon the peasant woman what she thought to be a bit of the seamless robe of her Lord, a portion of his Calvary cross, and a segment of one of the coins for which he had been sold. Still later when we removed the supposed relics we found a fragment of mother-of-pearl from a crucifix so old that the uncrossed feet of the Saviour indicated a design of Byzantine origin.

Before long Lane and I developed great respect for our small collection, regarding them not as fetishes of discredited sacerdotalism but as opportunities to study expressions of faith of many seekers through many centuries. We saw them as helps that had strengthened people to endure the cross set before them in the hope of ultimately sitting down "at table in the kingdom of God." These symbols became scattered tesserae in the mosaic of the great reality of redeemed, immortal life.

> When I survey the wondrous cross,
>   On which the Prince of Glory died,
> My richest gain I count but loss,
>   And pour contempt on all my pride.

Then, too, we had caught the collectors' fever, discrimination soon outstripping avidity. At the same time we came under the spell of the bazaars.

Whoever has felt the spell of an Eastern bazaar, whether in the silver market of Damascus, or in the perfume stalls of Cairo's cobwebbed Khan el-Kalili, needs be reckoned only once. Their sights and their aromas enthrall. The ancient disreputabilities and ragged, shabby hangers-on add to the

Arabian Nights' atmosphere of the exotic experience. Nothing of our standardized Western world of nervous, hasty shopping. From Athens east, the act of buying is an adventure not to be entered into with indecent speed. The amber and jewelry stalls of musty old Istanbul's roofed-over bazaars are housed in crumbling palaces and mosques adjacent to odorous caravanseries where pierced-brass camel lanterns and woven saddlebags are redolent of the ancient East.

> I cannot describe, I cannot explain
> The thrill I get from a camel train.
> A camel train with burdens and bumps
> And beads and bells and laden humps,
> As it comes from the markets of old Baghdad
> With silks and rugs I should like to have had.
> A camel train, by a donkey led,
> A camel train with its tassels of red,
> A camel train on thistles fed,
> Yet stalking along with a regal tread!
>
> M.S.M.

The brilliant silk stalls of Arab Jerusalem and the sticky cocoanut sweetmeat shops on stepped David Street—who can forget? Or the rug markets of Cairo, where mellow old Kermanshahs and leafy Tabriz and Chiordes prayer carpets worn thin by Mecca-facing Moslems are carried out into dark alleys by desperate merchants who shout bargain prices and entice customers with proffered glasses of amber tea or cups of sweet, bitter coffee. Sad that the vine-clad Libyan silversmiths' bazaars are being modernized and crammed with bolts of Western yard goods.

So—the lure of the bazaars, the fascination of collecting treasures, the joy of adventuring together, and a deepening appreciation of the symbol we had chosen led us down many years and across many lands. Our collection enriched our own lives, and those of many others.

2

Everywhere the Cross

ONCE A person has begun a collection he may no longer be his own master. This collection sometimes takes control and threatens to dominate his leisure if not his pocketbook. Our study of symbols, which began with the purchase of the two crosses in Athens, has enhanced our interest in geography, geology, architecture, history, nature, religion. From the beginning we have consistently tried to verify the source of each piece we have added to our collection and in the process our respect for each piece has increased. Jordan, Israel, Syria, Greece, Egypt, Italian Ravenna, the catacombs of Rome—all have contributed to our attempts to reconstruct the radiance of the worshipers who developed the Christian symbols in their effort to make religion live "in spirit and in truth."

But more than that, wherever our eyes turn we see indications, reminders, of the cross; in churches, in nature, in other emblems—everywhere the world seems full of cross-shaped objects and symbols. As their significance has grown on us we have found the whole field of Christian iconography an enriching study and have been happy that we could incorporate some of the symbols into various churches we have served, especially the Hanson Place Central Methodist Church in Brooklyn, New York, constructed during our twenty-two-year ministry there.

After we had been collecting for some years we wrote a book on our treasures. Since then our personal collection has continued to grow. Also, new information has been acquired concerning some of its controversial items. Moreover, the ever-advancing science of archaeology has encouraged a few eminent scholars to express themselves as to when, where, and in what form the earliest crosses of Christendom were fashioned.

Along with this growing body of information is the growing interest of churches in traditional symbolism. Within the past twenty years many of the nonliturgical churches which were formerly opposed to, or at least disinterested in, placing a Christian cross on altar, reredos, spire, gable, or cornerstone have developed a satisfaction in the use of this chief symbol of their faith.

Christian scholars are discovering that the liturgy of the early Church was extraordinarily alive, rich, and designed to build up the body of Christ. They find, as Oscar Cullman has pointed out in his *Early Christian Worship,* that "the Revelation of St. John may be used as a source-book for the liturgical materials of early Christianity." Early Christian art also reveals a profound interest in liturgy.

The trend toward wider employment of crosses has led more people, both clergy and laity, to inquire into the various symbols which, taken together, constitute the subject

matter of Christian iconography. Many intelligent Protestants
are for the first time learning the difference between the
fundamental Greek, Latin, and Celtic crosses. They are in-
quiring what the Chi Rho (XP) on their altar signifies, or the
Alpha and Omega (AΩ) in a window they may have seen
since childhood.

A study of church architecture presents interesting cruciform designs. The five-aisled, triapsidal Church of the Nativity at Bethlehem, begun in the fourth century during the
reign of Constantine, suggests in its ground plan a trefoil
cross. Generally, cruciform churches tend to be of two types.
First, the one in which the whole edifice appears as a free-
standing cross, such as San Marco in Venice, completed in
the eleventh century, and copied from the no longer existing
Church of the Holy Apostles at Constantinople. Second, the
Greek cross type of church (*l'église à la croix grecque*),
which was the typical Byzantine form from the close of the
ninth century to the end of the Empire. Seen from the
ground, it looks like a square structure, inasmuch as auxiliary
rooms fill in the angles of the cross; but studied from the
roof or above the ground level, the square Greek cross is
plainly seen.

In a typical Byzantine church the central dome is lifted
by round arches and augmented by four other domes. Some
authorities believe that a Greek cross church was constructed
in Constantinople in the palace grounds of Emperor Basil I
(A.D. 867–86), and was called the Nea or New Church. The
typical square-cross Byzantine church is still in evidence at
Ravenna, especially in the charming fifth-century, so-called
Mausoleum of Galla Placidia.

An eleventh-century Byzantine church still stands in Athens in Hermes Street leading to Constitution Square. This Kapnikarea Church, dedicated to the presentation of the Virgin, is cruciform, surmounted by a dome. The name Kapnikarea is derived from the Kapnikarioi, meaning the donors of church funds, a title denoting tax collectors during the Byzantine Empire. Another Byzantine church surviving in Athens is the small Church of Panagia Gorgo-epikoos, adjacent to the Cathedral of St. Mary. Equally interesting in architecture is the cruciform tile-domed church of Daphni Monastery, whose interior is adorned with mosaics portraying the wide-eyed short-bearded Eastern Christ for whose head the aureole or nimbus is triradiant.

The successive architects who designed the fabric of the Basilica of St. Peter in Rome alternated between the ground plan of a Latin cross and that of a square Greek cross. Raphael's plan was in the form of a Latin cross; Michelangelo returned to the design of the Greek cross which had been planned earlier, in 1506, by Bramante. After the death of Michelangelo, in 1564, Carlo Maderno returned to the design of the Latin cross which was ultimately carried to completion after the edifice had been under construction for more than a century.

The pattern of the cross is not confined to man-made structures or symbols. Everywhere the cross looms for those who are alert to see it. In nature, it inspires us in the passion flower (*Passiflora cerulea*) that blooms on sunny walls enclosing the olive-shaded Garden of Gethsemane or is imported from tropical South America as an exotic Easter novelty. A crown of thorns appears to form the flowers in the corona, while the five sepals and five petals are said to symbolize the faithful Apostles—Peter and Judas being omitted—while other parts of the flower suggest the nails and the wounds of Jesus.

Some see in the dogwood an almost square Greek cross formed by its petals, with rust-brown "blood-stained nail-prints" in the center of the outer edge of each petal. Legend has attributed the flower to "tears shed by angels at the crucifixion of Jesus." Sometimes a gigantic cross of Easter lilies fringed by flaming azaleas may be seen in a city's conservatory.

The cross in nature is nowhere more beautiful than in the southern heavens where the constellation of the Southern Cross serves as pointer to the South Pole. Composed of five stars, one of the first magnitude, two of the second, one of the third, and one of the fourth, this constellation also includes nebulous clusters. The Southern Cross impressed discoverers and great navigators as early as the time of Amerigo Vespucci, Vasco da Gama, and Magellan. In terms of symbolism, the four main stars of the constellation denote the cardinal virtues: Prudence, Justice, Strength, Temperance; while the three pole-lighting stars represent Faith, Hope, Love. The constellation of the Southern Cross has been termed "The Advent Banner of the Explorers."

Crosses derived from nature are represented in our collection by one carved from the gleaming white native rock wall of Niagara Falls. Nature's seascape supplied coral for a delicately wrought Roman cross bought by Lane on a hill high behind the brilliant Bay of Naples. Another cross is drilled from Pennsylvania coal; a graceful Lithuanian cross is cut from amber or "northern gold"; a yellowing ivory cross cut from the tusk of an elephant or hippopotamus in a hot African valley is skillfully carved in the form of bundles of wheat, God's bounty.

Often we have been asked, "Do you have one of the Virginia 'lucky-stone' crosses found in natural rock? Are they genuine?" They are genuine natural crosses, appearing in Maltese, Latin, St. Andrew's, and Greek types, formed by staurolite twinned crystals of ferrous aluminum-silicate, a compound of aluminum, iron, silicon, oxygen, and hydrogen which, after they have "weathered" out or are "worked" out of the matrix, intersect in such a way as to form crosses. Actually they are found not only in Patrick County, Virginia, but also in Georgia, Minnesota, New Hampshire, France, and other regions.

The highest cross in the world is probably the gigantic 26-foot cross held by "The Christ of the Andes," a statue standing at 14,000 feet above sea level on the boundary between Argentina and Chile, reminding Argentines and Chileans that "sooner shall these mountains crumble into dust than shall the Argentines and Chileans break the peace which they have pledged at the feet of Christ, the Redeemer." Another huge figure of Christ, standing on a hill overlooking Rio de Janeiro with arms wide-extended somewhat after the manner of the Early Christian symbol of the *orans,* gives the appearance, when seen from city and harbor, of a gigantic cross. The highest cross in the setting of an American city tops the business skyscraper church which houses the Chicago Temple.

The largest cross in the world, its cost a million dollars,

has been projected by the American Federation of Women's Clubs. This structure is to rise on Bald Knob Mountain in southern Illinois, to house worship centers for all the major Christian faiths, and to be the base of a gigantic cross. Paths of approach will be paved with stones from the Holy Land.

The loftiest-appearing cross is a small Latin one which tops the gable of a little log chapel at Jackson's Hole, Wyoming. Viewed from a certain position which challenges a camera, this tiny cross looms against the Wyoming sky in such a way that it looks higher than the jagged, snowcapped Grand Teton peak behind it.

The lowest cross in the world is in the subterranean salt of the Cathedral of Zipaquirá in an ancient mine forty miles north of Bogota, Colombia. A cathedral as large as Notre Dame in Paris is being built inside the ancient mine which was old when Spaniards came to this region four hundred years ago, and a gigantic floodlighted rock-salt cross is silhouetted against the wall of the main nave. More than two hundred thousand persons each year visit this cross-centered salt mine cathedral.

Lovely in its outdoor setting is the Old Rugged Cross on the Altar of the Nation in the Cathedral of the Pines in the White Mountains near Rindge, New Hampshire. In sturdy simplicity it looms against a reredos that is half blue sky and half the long gradual sweep of blue Mount Monadnock. The cross is a worthy memorial to Americans who gave their lives in World War II.

Once in the ruins of Tekoa of Amos, in the wilderness desert southeast of Bethlehem, we saw a Byzantine baptismal font standing out among the vestiges of this Old Testament town. The font is ornamented with stars and crosses. That afternoon, as we rode our donkeys back up to Bethlehem's Church of the Nativity, we remembered that on the roof of this well-loved church stars *and* crosses loom above the long-accepted traditional birthplace of Jesus, whose coming into the world incarnated the principle of the cross. It is significant that a cross, rather than a star or a manger, became the chief symbol of Christianity.

The historian Arnold J. Toynbee has given us a tremendous symbol of modern man and his relation to the cross of Christ. In the October 18, 1954, issue of *Time* an article tells of his seeing himself in a dream, holding precariously to a cross such as he had observed in the Abbey of Ampleforth. As he clutched the cross desperately, a voice seemed to say *"Amplexus expecta!"* "Cling and wait!" Possibly the ultimate message of historian Toynbee is couched in this vision of a modern man clinging to the cross while he makes every effort to maintain himself and wait out his time.

The ubiquity of the cross includes the emblems of honor given in recognition of great courage. In the United States, the Distinguished Service Cross of the Army is a square one, circled with the sign of eternity and carrying at its center an eagle. The Navy Cross resembles the Canterbury or consecration cross, square with rounded ends, and having bundles of light rays, signifying immortality, shooting from the intersection of its arms. The Distinguished Flying Cross, reminiscent of the Bethlehem cross, is a cross pattée with squared-off bundles of light rays, carrying on its upper surface a square cross formed by the propellers of an airplane. In other lands, too, the cross appears in government decorations, as in the German Iron Cross and Hitler's Mothers' Cross.

The cross of the British Chaplains' Corps embodies three crosses, including a Maltese and a round-ended square cross surrounded by the words, "In This Sign Conquer"—dating back to the insigne on the battle standard of Constantine the Great. British civilian Orders of Knighthood, such as "The Most Noble Order of the Garter," usually incorporate a cross on their badges. But decorations of honor belong rather in the category of heraldry than in the field of Christian iconography.

The royal crowns of England from the time of Henry V and Charles I down to the era of Queen Elizabeth II lift high the cross pattée or some other form of Christian symbol. Embodiment of the Christian cross may be studied in sumptuous crowns of historic significance—those of Charlemagne, of St. Stephen of Hungary, the Crown of the German Empire, and the Great Imperial Crown made by the court jeweler Posier for Catherine II in 1762, topped by a cross of superb diamonds supported by a tremendous uncut ruby. Royal scepters are often topped by crosses, as are the orbs of British rulers—the orb being a golden ball surmounted by a jeweled cross, signifying the sovereignty of Christ over the whole world.

The flags of several nations also embody crosses. The Union Jack of Great Britain carries the X-shaped St. Andrew's cross, with the X-shaped St. Patrick's cross (red on white), as well as a square cross intersecting it. The flag of Norway has an unequal-armed blue cross on a red field. The flag of Greece carries a square Greek cross in white against a blue field. The flag of Switzerland embodies a square white cross, reverse of the Red Cross symbol. Finland, on its merchant flag, and Sweden on its man-of-war, incorporate crosses.

In the philately of the nations, crosses appear. In Italian issues of 1926 and 1929 crosses are seen among Romulus, Remus, and the wolf of Rome; exquisite crosses appear on Italian stamps of 1932, one in conjunction with the dome of St. Peter's, and one circled cross embodying angel wings. Eastern crosses are seen on 1926 and 1929 stamps of Latvia and Lithuania. In 1935–36 Rumania included a Christian cross in her stamp designs, as did Portugal in 1931. Spain in 1930 issued a dramatic stamp showing a huge-sailed galleon protected by the cross. Maltese stamps usually embody the eight-pointed cross characteristic of this island. New Caledonia, New South Wales, Nicaragua, Peru, have from time to time issued cross-bearing stamps. Switzerland, from 1854 on, has frequently used the square Christian symbol on her stamps. In 1933, the anniversary of Sir Humphrey Gilbert, inventor of the safety lamp, Newfoundland issued an anchor cross having on top of it something which looks like his safety lamp. About 1929 Czechoslovakia issued a stamp on which a cross bears witness to the Christian faith of that country. Greece, during years of occupation in 1913 and 1922, placed crosses on stamps. In 1934 Germany printed a stamp emblazoned with the swastika, the hooked cross used by Nazism as its symbol. In 1938 French Equatorial Africa, known as Free France, placed a form of the Christian cross on a stamp. A valuable Belgian stamp carries a double-barred Lorraine cross on the shield of a horse-mounted

Crusader to commemorate the leader of the First Crusade, Godfrey de Bouillon, who sold his castle in the valley of the Semois and left his possessions to follow Christ.

The cross is also incorporated in the design of coins. As early as the era of Constantine the Great in the fourth century, crosses began to appear on minted money. Lane's coin collection includes an "M" denomination bronze one issued in 537 by Justinian, builder of Hagia Sophia, which carries several perfect types of the Byzantine cross. Another cross-bearing coin was minted in the sixth century by Maurice Tiberius, an Eastern emperor at Constantinople, in the thirteenth year of his reign. A silver florin (two shillings) issued by King George V of England carries an impressive square cross emblazoned with symbols.

Since the Metropolitan Museum of Art in New York purchased a hypercubist painting of the Crucifixion scene by Salvador Dali, the world is even more interested in the "shattered gold cross," called by its designer "The Light of Christ." This gold cross, lighted by a sunburst explosion of six hundred diamonds piercing the Latin cross, and three rubies symbolizing blood-drops, expresses the artist's protest against the current lack of spirituality which, he feels, threatens quite as much as the hydrogen bomb to exterminate the universal artistic heritage of past as well as modern art.

Many feel that the cross is part of God's design for the universe—a universe whose focal point is Christ's body "on the tree, that we might die to sin and live to righteousness."

❧ 3 ❧

The First Christian
Crosses

THE QUESTION as to when, where, and in what form the first Christian crosses were used has long interested Christian iconologists. Many scholars decline to express themselves, a conservatism characteristic of experts. Others venture opinions at the risk of having to revise them.

In the Bible the number of references to the cross is surprisingly small, even when the great figurative and exegetical passages are included, such as Mark 8:34: "If any man would come after me, let him deny himself and take up his cross and follow me."

One of the most impressive passages about the meaning of the cross in Christian discipline comes from Paul. A passage in I Corinthians may be an admission that the reason he failed to gain converts to the Way when he spoke to the Athenians of the Areopagus was that he failed to speak of the heart of the Christian gospel, substituting philosophy for the cross. This idea is borne out in his later letter to the

Corinthians: "When I came to you, brethren, I did not come proclaiming the testimony of God in lofty words or wisdom. For I decided to know nothing among you except Jesus Christ and him crucified." He stated boldly to the busy people of the Isthmus city, "Jews demand signs and Greeks seek wisdom, but we preach Christ crucified, a stumbling-block to Jews and folly to Gentiles, but to those who are called, both Jews and Greeks, Christ the power of God and the wisdom of God" (I Cor. 1:22 ff.). Paul viewed the cross as the force which reconciled men to God, "bringing the hostility to an end" (Eph. 2:16). He declared, "But far be it from me to glory except in the cross of our Lord Jesus Christ, by which the world has been crucified to me, and I to the world" (Gal. 6:14).

The author of Hebrews also stated concerning "Jesus the pioneer and perfecter of our faith" that it was he "who for the joy that was set before him endured the cross, despising the shame, and is seated at the right hand of the throne of God" (Heb. 12:2).

As to the place of the first cross of Christendom—the cross as fact, not as symbol—again the Gospels give evidence. Matthew 27:33 named it "a place called Golgotha (which means the place of a skull)." Mark 15:22 reads similarly, and by inference verse 30, "come down from the cross," suggests its location on an elevation, although "down" might refer merely to descent from the instrument of torture. Luke describes the scene of the Crucifixion, as does John, in words that parallel Mark's. The characteristics of Golgotha are met by the low knoll with its eye-socket, cavelike openings at Gordon's Calvary and the Garden Tomb. But as to its exact location, we most seriously consider the site of the tottering Church of the Holy Sepulchre, begun in the fourth century by Helena, mother of Emperor Constantine, referred to as the first woman archaeologist because of her search for the true cross of Christ. The site of Calvary was probably outside the first-century city wall, not inside as this church is today.

At any rate, we know that Calvary (Golgotha) was near the city, close to a traveled road, for Matthew records, "And those who passed by derided him, wagging their heads and saying . . . 'If you are the Son of God, come down from the cross'" (Matt. 27:39 f.). The author of Hebrews states, "So Jesus also suffered outside the gate in order to sanctify the people through his own blood" (Heb. 13:12).

The New Testament has little to say about the form in which the actual cross of Calvary was fashioned. It was a cross capable of being carried by one man, for "Jesus . . . went out, bearing his own cross" (John 19:17). Yet it was too heavy for a lash-weakened man to carry even to a low hillock, so "they compelled a passerby, Simon of Cyrene, who was coming in from the country, . . . to carry his cross . . . to the place called Golgotha" (Mark 15:21 f.). Luke and Matthew record the same story. Some scholars believe that upright beams were left standing on the low hill at the place of Jerusalem crucifixions, and that Jesus carried a six-foot crossbar on his bleeding back. The beam then was attached to the upright by a long spike.

There is no certainty as to the shape of the cross on Calvary. How far up on the perpendicular beam the transverse was nailed is not known. Probably it was fastened in the position easiest for the executioners to reach. If it was attached at the very top, a T-shaped or Tau cross which had been used in ancient times would have resulted. If the lower limb of the cross was longer than the part above the crossbeam, it would have been what later was called the Latin cross. If the point of intersection came nearer the center of the upright the result would have been what is known as the Byzantine cross. If the transverse was as wide as the upright was tall, the effect would have been that of an equal-limbed cross, later considered as one form of the Greek cross.

It is evident that the trilingual sign which Pilate wrote "in Hebrew, in Latin, and in Greek" must have been attached to the uppermost part of the cross, or to an additional transverse bar. If the latter was the case, the Calvary cross may have been the prototype of Eastern or Russian crosses, especially if it had a suppedaneum or lower bar on which the feet could rest, or to which they were nailed or tied.

Legend runs that the suppedaneum of Jesus' cross was twisted from its normal position to an oblique one, either by the writhing of his feet in agony or by the convulsion of the earth during the Crucifixion. Iconologists attribute the slanting lowermost bar to the effect of primitive perspective, following Byzantine rules of art.

Although the actuality of the cross is part of historical Christianity, the cross also as a symbol of that faith came early in its development. When Jewish believers were added to the Way the cross was not openly stressed for fear of offending new converts from the race which, as Matthew tells, through their chief priests and elders "took counsel . . . to put him to death." It is little wonder that Golgotha's tragedy was still a "stumbling-block" (Gal. 5:11) to many Jews. But "Christ crucified" was also folly to some Gentiles (I Cor. 1:23), although "to those who are called, both Jews and Greeks," the crucified Jesus was "the power of God and the wisdom of God."

So the cross, as symbol, was probably submerged after what may have been a very early use, first, because of consideration for Jewish Christians; second, to safeguard the life of Gentile believers during the persecutions incited by Roman emperors prior to the Edict of Milan, legislating toleration in A.D. 313. Also, it must be remembered that the cross was viewed as an instrument of shameful punishment under the aegis of Rome. Christians preferred to glorify the founder of their faith rather than emphasize his shameful end.

The failure of some Western Church Fathers to emphasize the cross as a symbol may be due to their having scarcely come under Paul's influence. However, Eastern apostles, who felt Paul's influence early, stressed liturgy and symbols. Many early Christians signed themselves with the cross upon rising and retiring, and upon the completion of important events during the day. Barnabas, a converted Jew and a Pauline Alexandrian who lived around the end of the first century, is mentioned as one of the first to attach a sacred meaning to the cross, regarding it as the distinguishing mark of the Christian, as circumcision was of the Jew.

If no definitive statement can be made as to the exact date or place of origin of the cross as a Christian symbol, this does not mean that records of its early existence are meager. The Index of Christian Art at Princeton University lists at least one thousand early representations. The vast file of this

Index occupies almost a floor in the south wing of the Department of Art and Archaeology, with iconographic material covering the period from the Early Christian Era to the year 1400. Duplicate copies of the Subject File are preserved at the Metropolitan Museum of Art in New York, and in Washington, D.C., at the Dumbarton Oaks Research Library of Harvard University. By an ingenious photographic device, an apparatus has set up photographs of the objects and monuments described in the Subject File. A staff of research experts is maintained to look up and to record data requested by scholars. Such is the amazing interest in the study of the cross and other symbols of Christian faith and experience in our own day. But no concrete dating of crosses seems available before the second century.

An eminent scholar, Professor Homer Thompson of Princeton, states in a letter, "The cross appears frequently on architectural sculpture of the fifth and sixth centuries. I enclose photographs of crosses found on Agora pottery of this era. But I know of no example in Athens that can be dated with certainty earlier than that. It is generally believed that the earlier representations of the cross are to be found in *Syria* and date from the end of the second or beginning of the third century."

This opinion is consistent with what is known historically of the early believers in the Way—"in Antioch the disciples were for the first time called Christians" (Acts 11:26). Evidence of the existence of a substantial company of Christians at Antioch is found in such passages as Acts 11:19 ff., where we read that those believers "who were scattered because of the persecution that arose over Stephen traveled as far as

Phoenicia and Cyprus and Antioch, speaking the word to none except Jews"; and in the statement that when the church at Jerusalem heard of the large numbers that believed and turned to the Lord, "they sent Barnabas to Antioch" and "a large company was added to the Lord. So Barnabas went to Tarsus to look for Saul; and when he had found him, he brought him to Antioch. For a whole year they met with the church, and taught a large company of people." We are told that famine relief was sent from Antioch "to the brethren who lived in Judea . . . sending it to the elders by the hand of Barnabas and Saul."

It would be expected that early Christians at Antioch might be among those who fashioned some of the first symbolic Christian crosses. Evidence of abundant Christian art is supplied by the wealth of iconographic materials discovered in Antioch-on-the-Orontes and its seaport, Pieria, by expeditions which went from Princeton to study remains of early Christian churches there. Volumes of evidence, derived from structures built in the early Christian centuries, have now been published. Such art works as the group in which the Antioch Chalice was discovered, dated between the third and sixth centuries, and the processional cross found near this same treasure, further support Antioch as one of the earliest centers where crosses of Christendom had liturgical use.

The view favoring Syrian origin of earliest crosses of Christendom is fortified by a writer in *Le Dictionnaire d'Archéologie Chrétienne et de Liturgie*, Volume 3, Part 2, who states his belief that the first representation of the cross on a Christian monument is in an inscription found at Pal-

myra, 140 miles outside Damascus on the Arabian Steppe in
the fabulously rich trade center of ancient Syria. The symbol appears twice, framing the date "month of Nisan of the
year 447," or April, A.D. 134, on a small altar dedicated "To
him whose name is blessed in Eternity!" The inscription
states that the altar had been made by Salmon, son of Nesa,
son of Tsaida, for his health and that of his children. The evidence is scanty. But the location is likely.

Another scholar whose opinion carries weight in estab-
lishing the time and place of the earliest-known Christian
crosses is Professor Amadeo Maiuri, Superintendent of Antiquities in the Campania, with headquarters at Naples, seat
of one of the greatest museums of ancient art in the world.
Professor Maiuri is best known for his work of many years
directing excavations and restorations at Pompeii and Herculaneum, buried under a stream of mud from Vesuvius in
A.D. 79, and at Ostia, ancient port of Rome. When queried as
to whether he had found any early Christian crosses in his
excavations, Professor Maiuri sent two glossy prints of a
crude metal cross found in 1938 at Herculaneum in a small
room of the house called the Casa del Bicentenario, and
wrote: "The above-mentioned town was hidden by Vesuvius'
ashes during the eruption in the year 79 after Christ. The
approximate date of this cross is about ten or twelve years
before the eruption."

The cross looks like a T-shaped or Tau cross, or possibly a
Latin one of which the upper portion of the upright extends
only a small distance above the intersection of the arms.
Possibly a part has been broken off. This cross is fastened
to the wall of a small room above what appears to be a
wooden altar having a basin in which offerings were laid, to

be cooked by a fire placed under it. The stone in the fore-
ground suggests a *prie-dieu,* where worshipers could kneel
before the cross.

The opinion of some critical scholars discredits Professor
Maiuri's first-century cross. One identifies it as a metal
"bracket." But there were certainly Christians living in the
Campania in the first century. Why not then at Pompeii and
Herculaneum? This region on the Bay of Naples is not far
from Puteoli where Paul landed for Rome, was met by
Christians, and was "invited to stay with them for seven
days." We see no reason why there may not have been cross-
using Christians in Herculaneum when the town was destroyed.

There is evidence that Christians were buried in Roman
catacombs at least as early as A.D. 170. In the Catacombs of
S. Sebastiano, a Christian burial ground developed over a
pagan cemetery, the names of Paul and of Peter are found
more than one hundred times. In fact the local belief is that
the Apostles were buried temporarily in this catacomb during persecutions under Valerian in the third century.

A recent contribution to the art of the cross comes from
new findings since 1949, under the Old Crypts at St. Peter's
in Rome, and include a tall, austere Latin cross that is said to
be unique in sepulchral art. It is standing starkly foreboding
behind a seated figure of Mary holding a beautiful Child,
both attired in graceful drapery. Three gift-bringing Magi,
whose camels are in the background, are bringing offerings
for the Child, whose arms are outreached to receive them.
Here is a Christmas scene, from perhaps A.D. 340—but with
the staggering warning of the towering cross in the background.

Other locations of early Christian groups include France, in whose Rhone Valley Christians had settled by the middle of the second century. Also Germany, Cologne, and Mayence, if we accept the inference of Irenaeus, had bishoprics before the end of the second century. Spain claims Christians early in the second century. And there is evidence that Carthage had its greatest increase in converts under Latin influence in the first half of the third century. Egyptian Alexandria also exerted a strong and early influence through its Christian literature and art.

Early Christian symbols, then, were profoundly influenced by Hellenistic thought and were spread by Syrians—characterized as being "the most highly endowed Semitic people"—people who, like the Greeks, were inveterate travelers and merchants. Leaders disseminated inestimable influence from schools at Edessa. The influence of Persian religious art also manifested itself in Early Christian symbols, as is indicated in motifs of some of the crosses.

In pondering the various regions where crosses first appeared as Christian symbols, we must not forget that some of the earliest Christian centers were Greek towns in Palestine, one of the most important of which was Caesarea on the Mediterranean coast, now under exploration by Jewish scholars.

The old feud between the early importance of East and West persists in the realm of intelligent Christian scholarship today. But, at any rate, the date for the early symbolic use of crosses of Christendom seems to have been pushed farther back than formerly. One of the possibly oldest existing specimens of the depiction of a Christian crucifix is on ivory plaques from a casket in the British Museum. The arms of

Jesus are spread wide upon his cross, as is so often the case in Early Christian representations of the *orans*, person praying with widespread arms, sometimes viewed as symbolic of martyrdom. Very early representations of the cross also appear on glass ampoules, or phials, brought by pious pilgrims from Jerusalem, filled with oil taken from lamps burning before shrines on holy sites.

Individuals making a collection of crosses will find it virtually impossible to obtain a cross from the earliest Christian periods. Today any that still exist are in museums or other permanent repositories. In our personal collection the two oldest crosses date, presumably, from the sixth century. One is a buckled cross found in a Crusader's tomb in Jerusalem.

Probably it is just as well that Christians will never know positively the exact location and form of the first symbolic Christian crosses. Certainty would no doubt lead to over-veneration of a place or to overstandardization of a type. As a symbol of the universal life-bringing sacrifice of Christ, the power of the cross cannot be restricted to any one form or any specific era or area.

The earliest Christians could never forget that some of them had witnessed Calvary. Others had heard the story from those who were present at Christ's last hours. Today the service of communion speaks to all Christians of the sacrifice on the cross. *The Book of Common Prayer* in the communion ritual reminds us that God gave his "only Son Jesus Christ to suffer upon the Cross for our redemption; who made there (by his one oblation of himself once offered) a full, perfect, and sufficient sacrifice, oblation, and satisfaction, for the sins of the whole world."

❧ 4 ❦

Perspective on Iconoclasm

THIS is an age in which people are relatively free to worship as they please. Therefore it is a good time to get a perspective on eras when the cross and other religious symbols were not welcomed and revered as sources of inner spiritual satisfaction.

In A.D. 313 after the official toleration of Christianity implied in the edict of Emperor Constantine the Great—sometimes called "the thirteenth Apostle"—groups of Christians felt safe in expressing their faith in as much pictorial symbolism as they desired. Worship came above ground into the sunlight which had been denied the candlelighted underground passageways of the catacombs along the Appian Way on the outskirts of the capital. There the early Roman Christians had met for worship and observance of the Eucharist, especially during the persecutions under Emperor Diocletian. Early symbolic decorations in some of the small chambers date from A.D. 200.

The trend toward symbolism developed early in churches of both East and West, as well as in the Coptic Church of Egypt. Early Christian art, always vital, was sometimes characterized by dazzling beauty, even when so-called European "barbarians" were in power. Thus the thirty-three years during which Theodoric the Ostrogoth ruled Italy (493–526) were spiritually prosperous years for Christians. Noble religious structures rose, some of which survive today. The Church of S. Apollinare Nuovo was built by him around the middle of the sixth century and designed to be the largest Arian Church. Its Byzantine mosaic friezes depicting saints, Magi bringing gifts to the infant Jesus, and a stupendous procession of Christian martyrs, cause modern beholders to bow in gratitude for survival of these masterful symbols of Christian faith. The Church of San Vitale, often called the high-water mark of Byzantine art in the West, was begun before the death of Theodoric; the decagonal, flat-domed mausoleum, erected by his daughter Amalasuntha, stands today illustrating one style of ancient Roman tombs.

When Islamic Arab conquerors humiliated Christians and Moslem domination swept through the Middle East from North Africa to Spain, Christians felt the contrast between their own representational art and the restful, geometric austerities of their Islamic conquerors. Indeed, many Christians associated their defeat with their own excessive use of icons and didactic religious pictures. Perhaps their Arab enemies had gained in resisting graphic representation of the divine personality. Other Christians of the invaded East resented the failure of Christian monks to participate in armed resistance against Moslem enemies who opposed images and pic-

torial representation of Deity. Constantinople was saved
from Islamic Saracens in A.D. 717 only by the fierce courage
of the Emperor, Leo the Isaurian, who destroyed religious
pictures, removed images, and plastered over the walls that
were painted with religious scenes. Such iconoclasm continued for one hundred and fifty years, during which many
Byzantine artists moved west to Europe, where their skill as
mosaicists expressed itself in Christian art which survives to
this day.

In the long struggle aesthetic and "geometrical" concepts
—abstract representations of ideas—became the vogue. Emphasis was laid upon use of floral motifs, richness of coloring
and textures. Truly, Christian art was influenced by the beautiful abstractions of Near Eastern religious art, seen today in
mosaics, marbles, and ceramic tiles in certain portions of the
sixth-century Hagia Sophia, in the eighteenth-century six-
minareted Blue Mosque of Ahmed in Istanbul, and in the
rich rugs which still cover the floors of many Moslem places
of prayer. Greek artists believed to have been summoned by
Caliph 'Abd-el-Melek to build and adorn the late seventh-
century prayer place in Jerusalem's ancient Temple Area,
known today as the Qubbet es-Sakhra, The Dome of the
Rock (often incorrectly called The Mosque of Omar), employed mosaics on a golden ground. The builders of The
Dome of the Rock made maximum use of abstractions of
marble, glass, faïence, to adorn the case which enshrines the
sacred Rock where, as many believed, David once built an
altar to halt a pestilence.

However, not all Arabs were iconoclasts. The Ommaid
Dynasty in the seventh and eighth centuries was not entirely

in sympathy with Mohammed's teachings, and maintained at Damascus a capital which did not hesitate to employ artists from any race or belief. Today the Great Ommaid Mosque at Damascus, once a Christian church dedicated to John the Baptist, is adapted for use as a Moslem worship center. With similar tolerance Caliph 'Abd-el-Melek rebuilt a church which had been a basilica erected by the Byzantine Emperor Justinian, known today as the Mosque el-Aqsa. It stands at the southern end of the old Temple Area in Jerusalem.

Although iconoclasm resulted in formalized symbols, as seen in floral motifs, stylized animals, stars, and other symbols observed in Eastern rugs, pottery, and textiles, yet it has left deposits of true abstract beauty that are timeless and restful. These abstract influences are reflected in some Christian Eastern crosses, as in the elegant Armenian cross and some of the Abyssinian crosses.

The historic iconoclastic controversy which rent Eastern Christendom for about one hundred and twenty years stemmed from attitudes of the Greek Christians who brought with them a belief in old pagan deities and faith in protective guardians—an idol worship which they channeled into Christian adulation of images. Emperor Leo the Isaurian inaugurated reforms but alienated many Greeks, some of whose monks were painters of sacred pictures. In 753 his son Constantine V summoned a General Council which condemned worship of images. Then in 787, the Seventh Ecumenical Council reversed the Iconoclastic Council and the struggle dragged on. Finally, in 843, one Theodora (not the wife of Justinian the Great), widow of Theophilus, restored icon worship and the debate ended. The Eastern Greek Church still observes "The Sunday of Orthodoxy" as the day of iconoclasm's formal condemnation. For a time, the Church at Rome and the Greek Church were in agreement, both suppressing image worship. But ultimately other arguments over papal supremacy and spiritual leadership rent Greek and Latin adherents apart. The permanent breach between East and West occurred in 1054 when Leo IX was Pope, and Michael Celularius was Patriarch of the Eastern Church.

In A.D. 732 at the Battle of Tours, Charles Martel drove back Arab Moslems who were pounding the West and Central France was spared such domination as Spain had suffered from the Moors. To Byzantine and Frankish armies we owe the survival of the great medieval sacred art and architecture which is our heritage in such centers as Rheims, Chartres, Amiens, Bourges, and Mont San Michel off the north coast of Brittany.

In the Middle Ages, during which some of the greatest cathedrals of the world were built, a bewildering amount of symbolism was employed. Saints and their emblems were depicted in stone and wood, on spires, sarcophagi, altar carvings, reredos, and cathedras, thrones appertaining to bishops. The emblems became too numerous for even regular worshipers to identify. Localities honored their spiritual heroes; religious history lived in dramatic form and crosses and crucifixes were conspicuous.

The Protestant Reformation of the sixteenth century was a revolution which again split Christendom. It is understandable that the Reformation both in England and on the Continent should have protested against mariolatry—excessive adulation of the Virgin Mary—and veneration of the cross of Christ as a magic symbol. Many legends began to be questioned, as, for instance, the one concerning the finding of what was claimed to be the "true cross" in Jerusalem in the fourth century, during a visit to Palestine by Emperor Constantine's mother, Queen Helena; also the legends about survival of "true fragments" in San Marco Basilica, Venice, and other shrines.

The great evangelical Protestant reformer Martin Luther advocated that joy be made the keynote of the holidays of the Christian Church, favoring celebration of many church festivals on Sundays and emphasizing the teaching of the New Testament and the institutions established in New Testament times. He regarded himself not as an innovator, but as one who relieved the Church from abuse and misinterpretations. In no sense an out-and-out iconoclast, Luther did not oppose the use of pictures in the church, for he felt that they had educational value; and he allowed the altar vestments and sacramental lights to remain. Many aspects of medieval liturgy were conserved by churches of his time, for he permitted individual bodies to establish their own form of divine service, so long as they retained essential aspects of Christian worship. Yet much of the spirit of early Lutheranism was actively iconoclastic, for it regarded symbolism as more or less characteristic of the Roman Catholic Church.

The rampant revolt of the English Puritan Oliver Cromwell, in the first half of the seventeenth century, was understandable as a protest against excessive pictorial representation of people and events termed sacred. But his iconoclastic brutality in destruction is another matter. One result of his influence was the inauguration of rigid austerity in church architecture, and the scantiness of pictorial aids to worship. In all, his reforms were devastating to religious art.

Nevertheless, religious art as an aid to worship has won its place. Canon Edward N. West of the Cathedral of St. John the Divine, New York, points out that at the consecration of an Orthodox bishop, the bishop is required to declare: "I reverence, relatively, but not in the way of worship, the images divine and reverence-worthy of Christ himself, and of the all-undefiled Mother of God, and of all the Saints, addressing to their originals the honour shown them. I reject as ill-advised those who think otherwise."

We can never cease to be grateful for the exquisite symbolic religious art left to us by artists and craftsmen of the medieval age, as seen, for example, in the newly arranged Early Medieval Gallery of the Metropolitan Museum of Art in New York, and in its branch, The Cloisters.

More and more Protestant churches are drawing on the treasures of symbolism. For instance, in a church built under my husband's leadership, much use was made of the symbol of the cross, with the intent of leading people to an understanding of the cross of Christ. From the communion rail their eyes are lifted across the chancel to the gleaming white limestone reredos behind the altar upon which the brass Jerusalem cross rises. On the face of the altar is carved a consecration or Canterbury cross, a square cross bounded by a circle of immortality. In the Resurrection Chapel the resurrection cross is used, a Latin cross the intersection of whose upright and transverse arms is shot through with a bundle of light rays, denoting eternal life. On the altar of the children's Bethlehem Chapel there is a Jerusalem or Crusaders' cross of olive wood, imported from Jerusalem. Sanctuary doors are studded with nailheads in the form of crosses. The metal door of the records repository is embossed with thirty crosses from historic settings. The Jerusalem cross is on cornerstone and gable. But most eloquently the cross is used to provide the pattern for the chancel flooring, in which are set stones gathered from Bethlehem, the Sea of Galilee, Calvary, Constantinople, Assisi, Epworth, City Road in London, and other places.

The symbolism of a great church is designed to lead those who meet there into the realms of the eternal, so that they inherit what John Ruskin had in mind when he said that we ought to build as if we were building for all time. In any church which is enriched by symbols, the meditative are likely to find words of some of the great hymns of the cross recurring to mind, as Thomas Tiplady's:

> Above the hills of time the Cross is gleaming,
>> Fair as the sun when night has turned to day;
> And from it love's pure light is streaming,
>> To cleanse the heart and banish sin away.
> To this dear cross the eyes of men are turning
>> Today as in the ages lost to sight;
> And for the love of Christ men's hearts are yearning
>> As shipwrecked seamen yearn for morning light.

Or it may be that some worshiper, arriving early for service, ponders the significance of the cross on the altar, or is caught into meditation by the mystic lights and shadows cast on the reredos by flowers and candles.

Modern religious leaders, like those of ancient Egypt who

were among the world's most eloquent users of symbolism, are constantly demonstrating the relation between religion and art. Although many worshipers find quiet satisfaction in a simple Friends meetinghouse where contemplation invites the Presence of God, other Christians feel that they need the symbolic aids offered by emblem, line, materials, and atmosphere of the liturgically enriched place of worship. They may never be privileged to see the superlative religious art of Hagia Sophia along the Golden Horn, or of St. Peter's in Rome, or of Notre Dame in Paris, or of Rheims, or Monreale Cloister in Sicily. But they can feel in their local church the radiance of a small jeweled window of hand-blown glass, or derive satisfaction from a sacrifical gift to the church in the form of a cross-incised Gothic pulpit in memory of someone who will forever live as long as Christ's good news is being preached from it.

Christian worship needs the fine arts. The symbols which we see before us as we lift our souls in the preparatory stages of worship bring forces of contemplation into action, lead us away from our preoccupation with the everyday mechanics of living, lift us out and up into the Eternal.

Alphabet of Christian Iconography

THE word "iconography" comes from two Greek roots: *eicon,* meaning "likeness" or "image"; and *graphia,* meaning "drawing," "writing." The representation may be painted or it may be wrought in enamel, stone, wood, ivory, mosaics, or some other medium.

The Roman catacombs are a primary source of information about Early Christian symbols. There, along the grass-blown Old Appian Way followed by Paul as he came in from the port of Puteoli, a traveler may halt, as did my husband and I on the tomb-lined outskirts of the capital within view of St. Peter's dome. Near a grove of eucalyptus and cypress we went down into the underground passages and chapels winding in a labyrinth of red brick walls, once marble and mosaic trimmed. During persecutions intensified by Diocletian the cult of martyrs became so popular that Christian burial vaults often became underground chapels, seating as many as sixty persons and arranged with higher places for clergy and a tomb adapted for an altar.

In the Catacombs of St. Calixtus, one of the most famous
of the Early Christian subterranean burial places, we saw by
the light flickering tapers *graffiti* or frescoes on stucco walls
and ceilings depicting the alphabet of Christian symbolism.
The ichthus or fish was used time and again. In the second-
century Crypt of Lucina, oldest part of this catacomb, the fish
is placed under a basket of small loaves and a glass of wine,
teaching that underneath the visible loaves and wine is
Jesus Christ. Christians sometimes use the fish as a symbol
for baptism but its most significant meaning comes from the
Greek words, "Jesus Christ, God's Son, Saviour," whose first
letters make the word "ichthus."

Another favorite symbol in this same cubicle of Lucina was
the Good Shepherd, symbol of Jesus carrying across his
shoulders a lamb, indicative of his nature. Again, the Shepherd appeared surrounded by a flock of sheep—the faithful
Apostles.

The *orans* (or *orante*) representing a person standing in
prayer with arms extended wide, palms uplifted, also typifies
adoration, the martyr, or sometimes the Church itself. A
ship also indicates the Church, transporting the faithful to
the home harbor. In the mast of the ship with its crossyards,
early Christians saw concealed a tall slender cross, looming
over all. A ship is included in the emblem of the World Council of Churches.

The olive branch denotes peace, healing, Noah, Gabriel;
gnarled: Gethsemane; the dove: the spirit of the departed,
or peace; the anchor: hope; the peacock with its renewal of
feathers: immortality; the stag: Christ; two stags: the Christian soul thirsting for baptism; the fabulous phoenix: the

Resurrection; the acorn: inherent strength or eternal life; the vine: the Eucharist, or the figure used by Jesus, "I am the vine, ye are the branches"; palms: victory, martyrdom, fields of Paradise, or Archangel Gabriel. For other symbols, see Glossary.

In our examination of the catacombs we found a hooked cross, a swastika or *crux gammata,* and a square Greek cross. One of the most interesting symbols was the Chi Rho, formed by the X intersected by P. The Chi Rho is based on the first two letters of the Greek word for Christ or for "the Anointed." This sacred monogram was affixed by Constantine the Great to his labarum or standard. During a difficult campaign he saw a cross in the heavens and immediately accepted it as the sign under which he would conquer. Thereafter the Chi Rho was carried by his bold legions into the little city of Byzantium when by a stroke of genius the Emperor chose this site along the Golden Horn to become New Rome, capital of a unified Empire far removed from the pagan politics of Western Rome. With the Chi Rho Constantine took another secret of the early Christians' power—the spirit of unity among those who had shared and survived a common persecution.

Some authorities claim that the Chi Rho monogram was used as early as the second century as an abbreviation of the Greek word for Christ. Certainly by the second quarter of the fourth century it was in common use. Frequently it was placed between an Alpha and Omega, the first and last letters of the Greek alphabet, signifying: "I am the Alpha and the Omega, the first and the last, the beginning and the end" (Rev. 22:13).

Walking one day along the River Arno in Florence in the shadow of the Ponte Vecchio with its array of silversmiths' shops near Benvenuto Cellini's bust, we came upon a push-cart of sundry trifles—jaundiced books, cheap jewels, broken pottery. And in their midst, a small brass lamp having for its handle a Chi Rho. For a lira or two we carried it off to join our collection of early symbols.

Up until a few decades ago it was generally supposed that prior to the fourth century the Greek and Latin crosses were not widely used. But in 1902 a scholar named Wilpert published a description of crosses in catacomb paintings; at least eight of these crosses he attributed to the first four centuries. One of these we recall seeing frescoed on the ceiling of a catacomb chapel.

The mind staggers when it tries to estimate the number of crosses in the world, each made because someone felt the symbol to be important and treasurable. One day in a church in Odessa we saw a young woman whose countenance was radiant. She was wearing a soldier's castoff coat. And in her worship she was using a cross and a rosary made from the raveled-out wool of a sweater, a symbol as effective for her purposes as any cross of enamel and silver.

Whatever they are made of, all crosses are derived from five basic forms. There is first of all the T-shaped or Tau cross, also called the pre-Christian or Anticipatory cross, because, with a loop added to the top to form a handle, it is identical with the Egyptian ankh or key of life seen in the hieroglyphics of ancient obelisks at Heliopolis, or currently observable in the Istanbul Hippodrome, or on London's Thames Embankment, or in Central Park, New York.

The second fundamental type is the Latin cross, with its upright longer than the transverse arm. This variety is usually associated with Western Christendom centering in the capital of the Roman Catholic Church. Yet even when Byzantine or Eastern Christianity prospered most—from the fourth century of Constantine the Great through the sixth century of Emperor Justinian, builder of Hagia Sophia—the Latin cross also was used.

The third fundamental type is the old square Greek cross, equal-limbed and looking very much like the plus sign. This form is associated with Eastern Christendom. Beauty-loving Hellenistic artists recoiled from the cruelty suggested by the literal Latin cross and preferred to indicate the sacrifice by a square cross decorated with conventionalized designs rather than by an agonizing, crucified figure. It is hard to overestimate the influence of Hellenistic Christians, whether in Jordan where we see ruins of churches which were altered from pagan temples in the fourth century, or in Rome itself. In 1939 Pope Pius XII wore at his crowning a square Greek cross emblazoned on his pallium (a ringlike band on his shoulders).

The fourth basic variety of cross is the one used by Eastern or Slavonic churches, especially Greek Orthodox and Russian Orthodox. These churches both use the upright crossed by three transverse bars, of which the top one is shorter than the main transverse. The lowermost crossbar, called the suppedaneum, is diagonal, supposedly wrenched from normal position either during the Good Friday earthquake, or by the agony of Jesus. Russian crosses tend to have the suppedaneum slant in such manner as to have its right end the higher. This same effect was sometimes achieved by the primitive perspective of Byzantine rules of iconography. Greek crosses sometimes have their suppedaneum slanting in the opposite direction.

The fifth of the five fundamental types of cross is the X-shaped cross of St. Andrew, so named because the fisherman of Galilee is said to have been crucified head downward on a cross of this sort. It is also known as the saltier and is used frequently in heraldic designs.

Some scholars list a sixth basic cross—the fylfot or *crux gammata,* popularly called the swastika, known to Germans as the *hackenkreuz* and to the Chinese as *wan dz.* Signifying "object of well being," this design appears in various ancient lands. Aryans particularly showed a fondness for it. In Scandinavia the swastika is sometimes called "Thor's Hammer." The symbol was found in an Egyptian temple excavated in 1954. American Indians also used the swastika. In this almost universal symbol there are variations: sometimes the arms swing clockwise, sometimes counterclockwise; sometimes each arm contains another small swastika; but whether simple or elaborate it is the same symbol.

Many more types of crosses are to be found including the barbée, botonée, crosslet, fitchée, and fleury. A student who cares to study the forms and variations of the cross will find that he is led into a demanding study, but a rewarding one.

One of the most satisfying groupings of Christian iconographic material we have found is housed in the Early Christian and Byzantine section of the Department of British and Mediaeval Antiquities in the British Museum, London. The objects here displayed help us understand how early Christianity made its way into many lands and gave rise to art as varied as were the skills and tastes of the cultures it encountered and vitalized.

Time and again we have been inspired by poring over the cases displaying Coptic linen tunics with purple crosses woven into the texture; or a silver basin from Cyprus with a nielloed Byzantine cross and a head of a popular Syrian martyr at its center. One would recognize this cross as emanating from Constantinople no matter where it might be found. There, too, are cross-trimmed silver spoons used in feeding the poor; Roman plates bearing the stamp of the cross recovered from a ship sunk in the Thames; finger rings of gold and silver, set with seals and intaglios of precious stones, bearing tender inscriptions, such as "Accept this present, O sweet One, and may it be yours for many a year"— probably a betrothal gift—and "Arborius, mayest thou live long in Christ." Two gold wedding rings, one from the fifth century, one from the tenth, are ornamented with the cross and scenes from the life of Christ which make the observer realize how vividly the Christian faith was a part of daily life in those glowing centuries so often set down as "dark."

The portrayal of Jesus himself came into use very early in the history of Christian art. In early Greco-Roman times it was a vital, wide-awake *Christos*; short-haired and beardless. By the first half of the third century he was represented with a short beard and a gentle expression, as is seen in one of the catacomb chapels. By the fourth century he was a fully bearded figure. The variety of the representations of Christ we saw portrayed in the catacombs convinced us that the early painters had no authentic portrait of Jesus.

It is notable that on the Chalice of Antioch at The Cloisters, New York, dating between the third and the sixth centuries A.D., two depictions of Jesus are presented—one showing him in his youth, and one after his resurrection. Two groups of five men appear to be hailing Christ and each holds a scroll. Definitive identification of these ten has not been made. Are they New Testament writers, leaders in churches, saints, apostles, or "last prophets"? But the iconography of this "oldest known Christian chalice" is important.

The figure of Christ on the cross was not an early symbol. To the Jews, portrayal of the Messiah by a human figure savored too much of the idolatry against which they had been schooled by Moses. Mesopotamia, however, has yielded a painting, dating from about 586, depicting the Lord on his cross, wearing a long, sleeveless, purple tunic. The form in which the garments of Christ were portrayed offers a study in itself.

By the end of the seventh century the use of the crucifix was widespread. On the earliest crucifixes the figure of Jesus was only outlined. Later it was painted on wooden crosses; still later, embossed or superimposed in metal on wood. Not until the ninth century, in the time of Leo III, did a bas-relief of Jesus on the cross appear. The depiction of the Lord upon a cruciform panel is essentially Italian, though often considered Byzantine. It belongs to the pious art of medieval Italy, to that century which gave the world Francis of Assisi.

As a young man he was gazing on a Byzantine crucifix used as a reredos in the rustic chapel of San Damiano on the outskirts of Assisi when a sudden call came to him. It was a call to dedicate his strength, his ability, his enthusiasm, his wealth as the son of a silk merchant, to serving his Lord whose eyes seemed to meet his gaze as he prayed in the quiet of the tumbled-down shrine among the old gray olive trees of the Umbrian Valley. We, too, have prayed in that chapel of San Damiano and can understand its spell cast upon Francis, and later upon Clara, whose order of worshipful, diligent women he established there.

Young Francis saw in the crucifix of Albert Spezio not the bleeding wounds of a dying Saviour, but a living, vital Companion, challenging him to enlist in a life of endless service, poor in all things save joy and love. Immediately he began to rebuild the prayer place with his own hands, as a labor of love. In later years the famous cruciform panel which had transformed his life was transferred to the Church of Santa Chiara in Assisi, where today the devout Poor Claras draw back their curtains to show this treasure to curious visitors.

With the beginning of the thirteenth century, a more realistic treatment of the crucifix came into vogue, showing the drooping head, the tortured body of a dying Saviour.

A notable collection of Coptic and fourteenth-century French enameled crucifixes is to be found in the Metropolitan Museum of Art in New York. Deeply impressive is a thirteenth-century Limoges cross of metal and enamel. The body of Christ is hanging on a green treelike cross which rises above a skull symbolizing death and sin. Above his head is the Greek inscription for Jesus Christ. The Syrian gold necklace and crosses from the sixth century are lovely, as is the gold necklace from the third century, with pearl and sapphire pendants similar in shape to our own Coptic cross. Beautiful also is the Spanish book cover made for Queen Felicia of Aragon about 1083, ornamented with a cross surrounded by vines, studded with cabochons or very ancient stones; and the fourteenth-century square Slavic cross bearing at its center Christ rising from a chalice, with the archangels Gabriel and Michael at top and bottom, and two six-winged seraphim beholding.

Nowhere may one see such superb crosses worked into metal book covers as in the Pierpont Morgan Library in New York. A certain "Gold and Jewel Cover" of French work from the ninth century is ranked the "most finished specimen of Carolingian goldsmiths' work in existence." Embossed on that cover is Jesus on his cross, mourned by two holy women and his mother, with the sun, moon, and four angels beholding. The type of Christ portrayed is the living Byzantine one, his feet not crossed and nailed. He wears the loincloth, not the tunic. His head is not drooping in despair, but lifted, beholding the needs of those about him. His hands are uplifted, with two fingers extended in the Eastern form of benediction.

This collection also reveals rich iconographical details in the twelfth-century French work of silver and enamel; in German fourteenth-century book covers of ivory relief and silver; in a thirteenth-century Spanish illuminated *Commentary on the Apocalypse* by St. Beatus of Liebana; and in an illuminated Latin missal in fourteenth-century Italian work. All appropriate companions, these, to the ninth-century Gospels in Latin, whose entire text is written by an unknown French manuscript writer in letters of burnished gold on vellum in varying shades of royal purple—a kingly gift, indeed, presented to Henry VIII, "Defender of the Faith," by Pope Leo X. The copying was probably done in the Palace School of Charlemagne.

In recent times a new emblem incorporating a cross has been worked out by the World Council of Churches. Its *Oikoumene* symbol accepted by 163 Protestant and Orthodox bodies in forty-eight countries gives evidence of the extensive acceptance of the suffering of Christ for the redemption of the world and the power of the immortal stream of love which has flowed down from the cross since Calvary. *Oikoumene* is a Greek word meaning "universality."

The *Oikoumene* has as its basis an Early Christian symbol seen in paintings on damp walls of Roman catacombs. Dating from the age of persecution of Christians, it shows a small sailing vessel riding almost overwhelming waves, yet plowing through to its desired haven. The upright mast of the ship with its transverse yardarm forms a cross. This courageous emblem suggests man's long voyage over life's sea to eternity; it also denotes his universal longing to journey to far-off places, to find fresh horizons, to evangelize the world, and is growing in Christian grace.

W. A. Visser 't Hooft, General Secretary of the World Council of Churches, commenting on the appropriateness of the *Oikoumene* symbol, said that the churches all together form the *Oikoumene* which is the fellowship of the Churches of Christ, world-wide in scope and attempting to serve all men.

At the meeting of the World Council of Chrches at Evanston, Illinois, in 1954, the diversity in ecumenicity was evident in the various forms of cross worn by the delegates.

Metropolitan Juhanon of the Mar Thoma Syrian Church of Malabar, India, one of the most ancient churches of Christendom (established, so tradition says, by St. Thomas), wore on his veiled, tarbooshlike headdress several small crosses of the square type suggesting Syria; but he also wore on his gown, over his heart, a plain Latin cross. The delegate from Kottayam, India, a minister of the Orthodox Syrian Church, also wore embroidered square crosses on his flat clerical cap. The stately Greek Archbishop Athenagoras of Thyateira wore an impressive panagia or encolpion on a heavy silver chain. The Russian cross worn by the ninety-seventh Anglican Archbishop of Canterbury, Geoffrey Fisher, had been presented by the Patriarch of Moscow. A sweet-faced German deaconess, a delegate, wore on the apron of her garb a rather large Latin cross. Bishop Eivind Berggrav of the Church of Norway wore a large, simple Latin cross, for which his formal, pleated white neck ruff, à la Frans Hals, formed, undesignedly, a circle of immortality such as is incorporated in the design of many crosses. The cross preferred by the representative of the Coptic Church of Egypt, one of the world's oldest Christian bodies, must have been one of the several indigenous Coptic crosses. Bishop Otto Dibelius of the Evangelical Church of Germany, two-thirds of whose territory lies behind the Iron Curtain, wore over his high clerical vest a heavy-armed square Greek cross whose intersecting upright and transverse arms seemed to be shot through with bundles of light rays which make it a resurrection cross, not unlike one in our collection whose provenance is Istanbul.

Stained-glass windows offer another medium for Christian symbolism. In the Wesley Methodist Church of Worcester,

Massachusetts, the *Te Deum Laudamus* window incorporates the cross of a triumphant Christ; a six-pointed star, Old Testament, and a five-pointed star, New Testament or Epiphany; dove, divine grace; lamb, purity and mildness; tablets of the Law, burning bush, Moses; knife of sacrifice, Abraham; horn of anointing oil, Samuel; harp, David; sword, Paul; inverted cross, Peter; plumb line, Amos; tongs and coals, Hosea; broken chains, Isaiah; torch, Ezekiel; lion, Daniel. These and many other symbols may be found in such centuries-old cathedrals as Canterbury Cathedral, as well as in other modern churches, such as the East Liberty Presbyterian, Pittsburgh, Pennsylvania; St. Bartholomew's, New York; the Riverside Church, New York; and the Cathedral of St. John the Divine, New York.

Many rose windows that gleam above their altars incorporate, as does the one at Hanson Place Central Methodist Church, Brooklyn, New York, the emblems of the Twelve Apostles, with a cross denoting Christ at the center. Fine stone carvings of the Twelve appear above the main portals of the First Baptist Church in Pittsburgh, Pennsylvania. Symbols for the Apostles vary, but the following are common: Peter, two crossed keys making an X (also an inverted cross and a cock); James the Greater, three scallop shells (pilgrim emblem) or a pilgrim's staff and hat; John, a chalice from which a serpent rises, or a serpent and sword, or a scroll of his Gospel; Philip, a cross with two loaves of bread; Thomas, a carpenter's square and a spear; Bartholomew (Nathaniel), flaying knife on Bible; James the Less, a saw; Matthew, three moneybags; Jude, a sailboat or an inverted cross; Simon, numerous symbols, including a boathook piercing a fish;

Judas, a blank, yellowish shield; Andrew, an X-shaped cross; Matthias, book and ax.

The Bible itself is rich in symbols. The Sabbath and the rite of circumcision both symbolized covenants of God with Israel. The eight garments of the priest symbolized aspects of sanctity. Gestures were symbolic. So, too, were metals; silver denoting spiritual innocence; brass or copper, firmness, hardness, strength. From the post-Flood rainbow of Genesis, symbolic of God's promise never to destroy the world again by deluge, to the Lord's Supper, symbolic of Christ's atoning and abiding fellowship with believers, the Bible is a record of the development of symbols. This tendency reached its climax in the intricate symbolism of the Revelation to John, with its four horsemen, its living creatures, white horse and rider, "Faithful and True"; its beast from the sea; its seven bowls of wrath; its angel messengers; the superb imagery of the new heaven and the new earth; the healing of the nations; the holy city Jerusalem, with scintillating radiance, jeweled walls, and river of the water of life; the worshiping servants of the Lord reigning forever without need of lamp or sun in the realm where there is no more night, "for the Lord God will be their light."

As long as the Bible remains Christians will build their hopes and beliefs on their interpretations of its symbolism.

Saltire (St Andrew's)

Latin (Passion)

Tau (St. Anthony's)

Eastern   Russian Orthodox

Lorraine

Triple
(Papal)

Fylfot or Gammata

Celtic

Calvary (Graded Cross)

Byzantine

Anchor

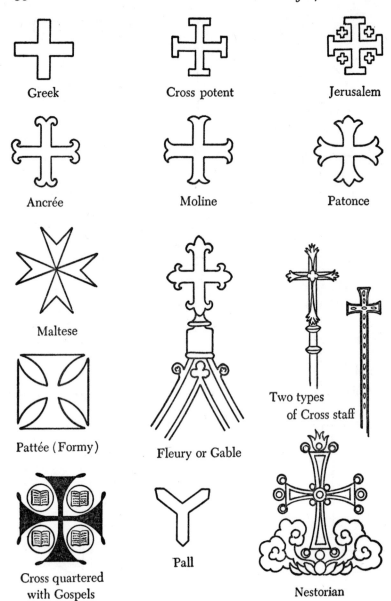

Greek   Cross potent   Jerusalem

Ancrée   Moline   Patonce

Maltese

Pattée (Formy)   Fleury or Gable   Two types
                                           of Cross staff

Cross quartered   Pall   Nestorian
with Gospels

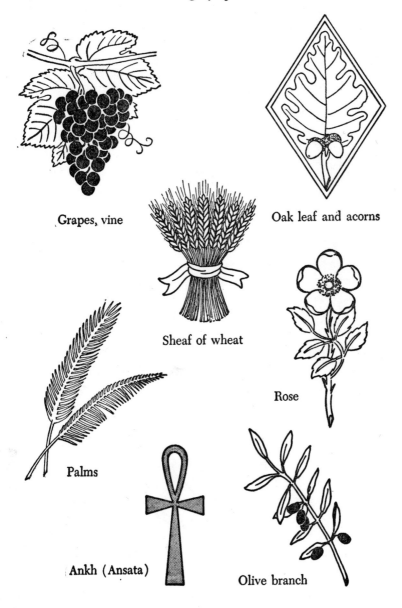

Grapes, vine

Oak leaf and acorns

Sheaf of wheat

Rose

Palms

Ankh (Ansata)

Olive branch

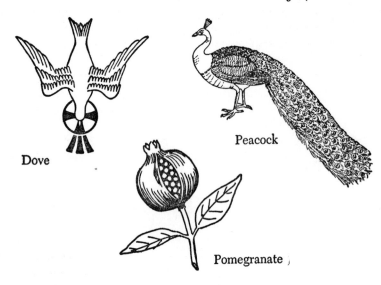

Dove

Peacock

Pomegranate

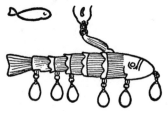

Ichthus

Christian lamp

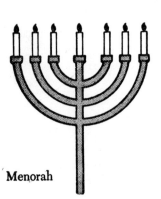

Menorah

Nimbus

All-seeing eye

Hand of God

Mariner's Cross

Good Shepherd

Sacred monogram
with Cross

Five-pointed star

Six-pointed star

Iesus Nazarenus, Rex Iudaeorum

Ecumenical symbol

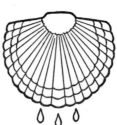

Shell

Jesus Christ, Victor

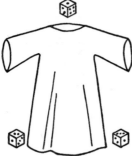

Seamless cloak, dice

Jacob's ladder

❧ 6 ❧

Crosses from the Lands of the Cross

TODAY THE Near East offers a rich variety of Christian crosses still available to anyone interested in the historical significance of the symbol or desirous of possessing a cross of ancient design. In the Kingdom of Jordan, in which Old Jerusalem is situated; in Lebanon and Syria, as in Anatolian Turkey and Egypt, individuals have in their possession—and merchants have for sale—crosses whose age and symbolic decorations make them desirable.

Our acquisition of a Crusaders' or Jerusalem cross is a treasured experience. After lingering in the shadowy intricacies of the chapels of the ancient Church of the Holy Sepulchre in Jerusalem we entered the sacristy to see the sword, spurs, and cross of Godfrey de Bouillon, elected the first Christian king of Jerusalem in 1099. We were intrigued by the design of this square cross, or cross potent, with a small square crosslet in each of its corners. Proceeding to our silver merchant, N. Ohan, in his shop by the Jaffa Gate, we inquired if he had a miniature of this historic emblem. The jeweler smiled as if an old favorite had been called for.

"I once sent my silversmith down to the Church of the Holy Sepulchre to draw the design," he replied. "Here is a copy reduced in size, but with exactly the same proportions as the original. Do you know its meaning? The large square cross represents the wound in the Saviour's side; the smaller crosslets, the wounds in his hands and feet, or the four quarters of the world for which he died. Or some say perhaps the five crosses represent the five principalities which made up the Latin Kingdom of Jerusalem; others, that the five crosses of the Jerusalem cross symbolize Christ and the four Evangelists; or again, the five nations who went to the Crusades to free the tomb of Christ from Moslems—England, France, Italy, Spain, Germany. Who knows? The large cross is of the crutch cross variety, a potent or an enabling cross, because the faithful one leans upon its strength and rebuilds his faith as he worships. Five rubies denote the wounds of Christ. This cross is sometimes called the cross cantonée. It was incorporated into the seal and arms of Jerusalem by the Latin kings of Jerusalem and it appeared on Crusader coins, those of Cyprus particularly."

How Godfrey came to choose this type of cross nobody knows. But we believe that one day he saw an Armenian cross and adapted it to his use, giving it richer symbolism. There are several similar examples in the Armenian Convent in Jerusalem. And in the rock-cut Convent Anée near Kars in the Caucasus, there was in the ninth century an Armenian crutch cross such as we today call the Jerusalem cross. Godfrey liked the old design, symbolic of pilgrims who lean on their crutches as they pray. Eastern Christians still stand as they worship, and many lean on their tall crosses.

Some authorities say that Godfrey also used the Lorraine cross, with its parallel arms, and consider it the true Crusaders' cross, but we believe that if Godfrey came to the Holy Land bearing the cross of Lorraine, he adopted this richer symbol of his Lord while there. Those who today call the cross potent the Jerusalem cross are in error.

The cross which we secured from Mr. Ohan is of careful Arab workmanship, studded with irregular oval red cabochons. It hangs from a chain of twisted silver, like those used by Eastern churches to suspend lamps.

Holding the Jerusalem cross in hand, we thought with profound admiration on that "best Crusader of all," for despite his critics, the humble Godfrey directed the siege of Jerusalem July 15, 1099, and entered the Temple Area, claiming it for Christendom. After declining the crown in favor of his brother Baldwin, he continued his work until, having contracted fever in the marshes of Huleh in northern Galilee, he died in Jaffa July 18, 1100, when only a little more than forty years old.

Appropriately Godfrey was buried under the site accepted in his day as Calvary, covered by the Church of the Holy Sepulchre which today treasures in its sacristy his Norman sword, spurs, and large pectoral cross. Wild Khwarazmians once marauded his tomb, but we know that originally it bore this inscription:

> Here lies buried the leader,
> Godfrey de Bouillon, who
> acquired so much territory
> for the Christian cause.
> May his spirit reign with Christ. Amen.

Today there is no tomb of Godfrey to visit in Jerusalem. But set in the paving of the court of the Church of the Holy Sepulchre, close by the twelfth-century Crusader portals whose pointed arches are dogtoothed with dentils, is the tomb of another good Crusader, Philip d'Aubigny, bearing on its stone slab a carved likeness of the long Crusader sword such as Godfrey used. Its hilt is in the shape of a cross. This type of sword was sought by European churches during the Renaissance for altar crosses.

The copy of Godfrey's cross is only one of the choice emblems we were able to purchase from Mr. Ohan. Always our visits to his shop west of the ancient city wall were high spots in Jerusalem journeys. Mr. Ohan was a Christian Arab whose wares were victimized by long disorders in the "Too Much Promised Land." He and his craftsmen who had inherited their skills from generations of Jerusalem silversmiths fashioned emblems of historic significance or exquisite pieces to suit the whim of a customer. For the wife of Viscount Allenby, liberator of Palestine in 1918 from four hundred years of Turkish rule, these designers created the Lady Allenby Chain, of delicate silver mulberries, grains of wheat, lamps, globules of lapis lazuli. For my husband they fashioned a ring, whose setting was of yellow gold, embodying the Bethlehem star and the Jerusalem cross. It held a Roman carnelian intaglio of the head of Jupiter.

At times, when the Church of the Holy Sepulchre became overstocked with pilgrims' offerings, old crosses hanging from massive silver chains reached this shop. Often we found that they embodied symbols from remote regions. Once Mr. Ohan gave Lane a twenty-four-inch, triple-barred cross covered with faded rose cloth adorned with stars and strings of crystals. This Eastern cross had long stood in a shadowy portion of the tottering Church of the Holy Sepulchre, where Easter worshipers saw it when they came for the Holy Season. Then, like many other pilgrim crosses from the East, it had been discarded. Lane cherished this iconographic treasure and kept it in a high place above his study desk through the years of his church building.

One year in Jerusalem we acquired two small bronze crosses which had been accidentally discovered in Crusader graves when workmen were excavating for a new house. One of these crosses became Lane's favorite in our collection. It may date from the sixth century. It is a Byzantine type and it hangs by a wide buckle which evidently attached it to the breastplate or belt of the Christian warrior. Since this cross antedates the Crusader by five or six centuries, we believe that it must have been acquired by its crusading owner on his way from Europe to Palestine to battle against the infidels. Or perhaps the Crusader secured it from a warlike Avar of Hungary.

Of course, we shall never know whether this particular Crusader belonged to the First Crusade whose members freed Jerusalem from Moslem rule, or to the unsuccessful Eighth Crusade of 1270. We shall never know whether he was among the Knights Templar, established to protect pilgrims; or belonged to the Knights Hospitaler who at first concentrated upon care of pilgrims who became ill on their journeys to Palestine, and later assumed military tasks, as at Rhodes. Imagination weaves its story when facts are not available.

The importance of the Jerusalem cross was recognized
when it was chosen as the cross of the Diocese and Cathedral
of Washington, D.C. to show that the Episcopal Church in
the United States descends not merely from Canterbury,
Rome, and Ephesus, but originally from Jerusalem. This
cross has also come to be regarded as the emblem of missionary work, the large cross representing the Church in
Jerusalem, and the smaller crosses the four corners of the
earth to which Christianity spread through missionary en-
deavor.

There is no doubt that the Crusades left a rich deposit in
the treasury of symbols. Much of the pictorial use of the
cross, however, belongs in the field of heraldry, rather than in
Christian iconography. Yet, as one thoughtfully climbs the
narrow Street of the Knights in Rhodes, he sees stone-fronted
houses which were once occupied by the Knights Hospitaler
of St. John of Jerusalem after expulsion from Palestine by
Moslems; he reads in the cross-emblazoned coats-of-arms the
record of their interest in freeing the tomb of Christ. Everywhere in Rhodes one finds the cross—this island itself having a distinctive square cross. So, too, in the island of Malta
one sees depictions of the eight-pointed cross of the knights.
And if one climbs the heights to the imposing Crusader
Castle, Krak-des-Chevaliers in Syria, there, too, in chapel or
on forgotten block of stone, one meets the cross-carving
propensity of the knights, as at Athlit, washed by Mediterranean waves that finally bore the adventurers in defeat from
this, their last stronghold in Palestine.

In architecture, also, the Crusaders left crosses in Palestine,
as in the pattern of the modern cruciform church which
tops Mount Tabor, one of the traditional scenes of the Trans-

figuration in Galilee. And in the churches at Emmaus, begun by Crusaders, their crosses are also found. Vestiges of their faith still loom in mosques that were once churches at Acre, Sidon, Tripoli; and at Ramleh, where their square tower survives. In Bethlehem, the dark steep steps leading down to the Grotto of the Nativity show crosses and mason's marks scratched by pious Crusader builders. As one journeys west he finds the reflection of the Crusader interest in crosses in Genoa with its church of San Lorenzo and its Tower of the Embriaci; in San Marco, Venice, which bears rich testimony to the religious art of the Crusades; and in the eleventh-century Cathedral of St. Andrew at Amalfi, one of whose citizens is said to have founded the Templars.

At length Jerusalem was lost to the Crusaders. Even the Templum Domini, the octagonal thirteenth-century prayer place which they had beautified because they believed it to be the ancient Temple of Solomon, was in the hands of the infidel. Still standing, however, is the Church of the Holy Sepulchre, part of which is the work of Crusaders. It embodies within its intricate shadowy structure holdings of several Christian bodies: Latins, Orthodox, Armenians, Copts, Syrians (Jacobites), Abyssinians (Ethiopians). The architecture of this church embodies a bewildering array of Christian symbols, many of them crosses.

The Latin type is represented in our collection by an austere tall silver cross left by a pilgrim in the Chapel of the Holy Sepulchre, a marble-encased structure containing "The Holy Tomb," with its fifteen ever-burning lamps, of which five belong to the Orthodox, five to Latins, four to Armenians, and one to Copts.

Greek (Orthodox) Christians are represented by our

square silver cross, studded with a blue stone from Medeba, east of Jordan—the small ancient town whose sixth-century mosaic map of Jerusalem in the floor of a church built by Greeks from Kerak, preserved valuable historical evidence of the streets and churches of an important era.

The cross of Bethlehem also comes from the lands of the cross. Bethlehem with a cross? Christians associate the star symbol with this radiant Judean town but it also has its cross. Our own silver one which I sometimes wear is a perfect specimen of the Bethlehem cross worn by Greek Christian matrons on the hand-embroidered bibs of their long-sleeved, flowing blue gowns. Bethlehem's history is so knit with the Crusades that memories of this medieval age still float about in the Frankish gowns and high tarboosh with voluminous white veil.

The Bethlehem cross suggests the *Croix de guerre*. Having an emblem in each of its corners, it is related to the Jerusalem cross. Each arm of its symbol terminates in a cluster of three palm leaves, symbolic of the Trinity, and of victory. Together, the twelve leaves stand for Christ's Twelve Men. Through the intersection run four spear points, reminiscent of the lances which pierced his side. The center of the cross has, like the corona of a passion flower, a crown of thorns and a sun, symbolic of righteousness. A concealed circle, eternity, completes the design. On the roof of Bethlehem's Basilica of the Nativity there are crosses of the three Christian bodies who control this well-loved church of Christendom which stands over the site of Christ's birth. But the symbolic star of him who became the "Life of the World" shines for all at the very entrance to the forecourt of the Church at Manger Square. It shines not only for the proprietary Latins, Greeks, Armenians, but even for their Moslem neighbors and for those of every faith and of no faith who come to Bethlehem.

The Bethlehem cross is also a representative of the Greek family of faith. Corinth on its Greek Isthmus contributed two silver crosses.

The Palestine Archaeological Museum stands today on the site of the focal point of the Crusaders' siege of Jerusalem in 1099. This storehouse of information about life and Biblical literature in ancient Palestine offers materials for the serious study of symbolism.

Among our most cherished crosses are two Armenian crosses. The Armenian Church is regarded as one of the oldest Christian bodies. Its adherents claim that the faith was first brought to them by the Apostles Thaddaeus and Bartholomew, and that as a people they were converted by Gregory the Illuminator, A.D. 301. The Armenian royal house adopted Christianity years before its toleration officially in Rome. The more elaborate of our two crosses is one of the most elegant in the group. Without any suggestion of a crucifix the Armenian cross is, of course, square, with trefoil ends typifying the Trinity. Small leafy designs in the four corners suggest the Jerusalem cross to which it is definitely related. Pendant from the three lower arms of the cross are lamps or decorated ostrich eggs. At its center is a blood-red ruby, surrounded by the twisted rope of eternity and a crown. The cross hangs from an elaborate chain, in which the grain of wheat alternates with the ostrich egg. The simpler silver cross of Armenian design resembles the Maltese, *ancrée*, surrounded by a leafy crown of immortal life.

The Armenian Christian Church developed a distinctive

form of art, as well as of ritual. As to the latter, the Armenian
Christians did not mingle water with wine at the Eucharist;
nor did they celebrate the Nativity as a feast but as a fast,
making instead a festival of the Epiphany. They broke away
from the Hellenistic representational art forms employed by
picture-loving Byzantine Greeks, and followed the Persian
penchant for Oriental geometric designs, flowing floral patterns, and animal symbols. They sympathized with iconoclasts who from A.D. 726, under Emperor Leo III, for one
hundred years protested against depiction of Christ and the
heroes of the faith. Armenian sacred art was plainly influenced by the Moslem Arabs who spurned everything akin
to idols. For several centuries prior to the Crusades, Moslems
and Christians intermingled, for the Moslem rulers of the
Holy Land allowed Christians to enter as pilgrims. In fact,
Greek artists may have been employed to collaborate in the
ornamentation of their Dome of the Rock on Mount Moriah.

One of our other prized crosses from the shop by the Jaffa
Gate is a Coptic one, reminiscent of the Egyptian Church
John Mark left as his heritage at Alexandria in the first century. This, like the Armenian, reflects a Persian influence,
based on conventionalized flowers which hang their blue and
silver beauty from the main cross, like cruciform florets. At
its heart is a slender mother-of-pearl cross surrounded by
tracery of pierced silver, from whose base dangles a Coptic
ostrich egg, symbolic of watchfulness—for as the mother
ostrich watches her eggs, so does Christ watch over his
Church. To Copts, as well as to Abyssinians, eggs which
hang from the chains of sanctuary lamps suggest the ancient
belief that the world was created from an egg. The old

Coptic Church sometimes used the ancient Egyptian hiero-glyph ankh or key of life for its cross. Medieval travelers to Jerusalem reported that Copts were there in small numbers and that their bishop wore a crown like the Greek patriarch's; and their monks, white pointed cowls. For centuries they practiced the ancient kiss of peace, and from shapely silver vessels sprinkled holy water on worshipers.

Today Copts are the Christian minority of Egypt. They claim descent from ancient Egyptians, some of whose words appear in Coptic liturgy. Thus the craving for eternal life of the ancient Egyptians anticipates the life-giving power of the Christian cross. For just as the Copts blended old Egyptian hieroglyphs with the Greek alphabet, so they fused the badges of Egyptian and Christian religions. The Coptic Church, through the centuries, has stressed the monophysite belief that God and Christ are of one nature. Their monks are energetic missionaries.

Our second Egyptian cross is a square bronze one found by our Arab friend Abdul when sifting historic sands near Memphis, once a thriving Christian community where now a date-palm oasis is strewn with temple fragments and grazed over by Egyptian heifers. The pious Copt who made it centuries ago retained the long loop handle of the ankh, but projected the upright to meet it. At the center is a deep round depression which may be intended as a circle of eternity; or it may be the setting for a lost gem. When urged to secure other Egyptian crosses, Abdul one day presented us with what he called a Christian cross. It is a bronze body of Christ which had become separated from the cross through the passing of centuries. His outstretched arms and upright

body form the true delineation of his own symbol. Good
Copts still face the East at prayer, seven times a day, and
they remember the cruel oppressions of the Emperor Diocletian by dating their important documents, not A.D., but so
many years after the Era of the Martyrs.

Certain Coptic crosses carved on Nile Valley limestone
tablets and tombs are full of primitive religious beauty, suggesting the asceticism of desert monasteries where Copts
early translated statements concerning the life of Jesus.
It is said that in the early Christian centuries there were ten
thousand monks at Egyptian Oxyrhynchus.

Garments found in Upper Egyptian tombs from the fifth
century A.D. show how the Copts used undyed linen and employed the tapestry methods of ancient Egypt. Jeweled
square crosses, symbolic birds, wreaths of foliage, fascinating bits of Coptic iconography are worked into their designs.
Cairo has a number of Coptic churches. From the Church El-
Muallaka, founded possibly as early as the sixth century, we
carried away impressions of a fine portrait of John Mark,
and of ivory and cedar inlaid screens, such as were used in
harems of palaces and early Coptic churches to separate
women and men. And in our camera we brought back lovely
crosses carved into a wooden lattice in the Museum of Coptic Art, adjacent to the venerable church. In the even more
famous Coptic Church of Abu Sarga, we were privileged to
see large crosses of solid ivory incorporated in the haikal
screen near the pulpit of inlaid rosewood.

In Coptic art, Christ is sometimes shown carrying a
scepterlike long-handled cross in miracle scenes, as the rais-
ing of Lazarus or the healing of the blind. This symbol of

power suggests the wand or rod influence of Moses smiting the rock.

Syrian Christians (Jacobites) have for their holding in the Church of the Holy Sepulchre, Jerusalem, a chamber near the Chapel of the Copts. In our collection the Syrian branch of Eastern Christendom is represented by several silver crosses acquired during visits to Damascus. One of these, purchased in the silversmiths' bazaar, indicates restrained Persian motifs, its pendants resembling palmettes in Eastern rugs. Its seller used his ancient fining pot to age a chain to match the cross. Another handsome Syrian cross from Aleppo has pendant coins hanging from the cross suggesting the relationship between one's financial resources and his responsibility for service.

The simplicity of our crosses from Syria is in line with traditions of local art which early parted from Hellenistic trends and turned to art forms of the Middle East. Her first Christian artists borrowed Mesopotamia's formal designs based on animals, vegetables, acanthus leaves, and palmettes. When they used human figures they resorted to inverted perspective, bringing to the front of a wedge the most important figure, such as Christ bearing his cross, with the lesser characters shrinking back.

When Syrians began to portray Christ on the cross they avoided the vivid manner in which pagan Greeks depicted their gods. Syrian artists represented Christ with reserve. The Syrian Christ wore a long soft beard and flowing locks parted above his noble forehead. He was fully clothed. They swathed Mary amply, as Fra Angelico did centuries later in madonnas at San Marco Monastery.

Another of our Near Eastern crosses is in the form of a cheap white enamel pennon, bearing a blue cross with a heart at the intersection of its arms. We accepted it because it was the only cross we could find to carry away with us from Lebanese Byblos, that old Phoenician seaport which gave us our word "Bible." The Republic of Lebanon offers many interesting Near Eastern crosses to iconologists. Most of them are colorful and modern, as seen in the busy shops of the harbor city Beirut.

For many years we had difficulty in obtaining an Abyssinian cross. The ancient Christian country of Abyssinia was betrayed by another Christian nation and in 1936 Emperor Haile Selassie was driven from his throne. Twice during this period, on the roof of Queen Helena's Chapel at the Church of the Holy Sepulchre in Jerusalem we interviewed the tall dark priests who served their pathetic colony, supported by gifts from African Christians under the tutelage of the Coptic Church of Egypt. Always they declined to part with their crosses, or to reveal where we might secure one. Indeed, they maintained a dignified exclusiveness in their hovels improvised from boards and cans.

Over each miserable door an Abyssinian cross was painted. One old priest, Gabriel, claimed more than a hundred years and remembered countless processions of Holy Week when swarthy pilgrims tented out upon the sacred roof and on Saturday night of Holy Week engaged in their ancient ceremony, "The Search for the Body of Christ." Every Friday, Gabriel told us, the Abyssinians fast because on that day Jesus was crucified.

A young acolyte led us to their chapel on the roof, above

the crypt where Queen Helena believed in that credulous fourth century that she had found the true cross of Christ and signaled the news by flares of fire up the coast and across the Mediterranean to her son, the Emperor Constantine. The acolyte, taking off his shoes with profound reverence, motioned us into the dark interior of the Jerusalem headquarters allotted to his people. It is a far cry from this chapel to the metropolitan churches and the Cathedral of St. George in Addis Ababa, capital of Ethiopia. But the little shrine contains a few treasures, including the famous tall crutch cross with its ivory handle.

A few years later in Jerusalem we met our Moslem friend Jacob, "Keeper of the Key," who at once led us to the shop of a Hebrew friend who brought out several choice Ethiopian or Abyssinian crosses, two of which looked as if they had been carved from the Maria Theresa thalers preferred by Ethiopian silversmiths for this purpose. One of the most typical of the three is a cross-crosslet of the type which tops the crown of Haile Selassie. The other one, crudely etched with a Christ on his cross, attended by Mary, John, and angels, suggests the general shape of the famous gilt-bronze Abyssinian processional cross in the British Museum, and the one presented by the Emperor to the National Cathedral at Washington, after Bishop Freeman had prayed for him on his coronation day in 1930.

Our third Abyssinian cross we received that day is the oldest in design, a simple pattée bearing on each arm the buds symbolic of the Ark of the Covenant, which the Abyssinians say was brought to their country from Jerusalem by Menelik I, son of Solomon and the Queen of Sheba! Among our other

Ethiopian crosses the most highly prized one belonged to Haile Selassie's son, the crown prince. He gave it to an American soldier, who upon his return to New York sold it to an antiquarian. It is made of silver coins showing the Lion of the Tribe of Judah, and a portrait probably of the Menelik who was predecessor of the present Emperor.

Ethiopians are proud of their relation to Semites. The coronation ceremony of Haile Selassie was a blending of Hebraic and Christian elements. "Blessed be the king of Israel" was chanted at the coronation of this, the "one hundred and thirty-fourth Christian King of the Empire."

Ethiopian crosses worn at a coronation are varied. Priests and royalty all wear them. They tend to be modified forms of the square variety. That on the Emperor's crown is definitely of Coptic proportions. The one which tops his orb is also a square cross-crosslet.

In 1954 a $15,000 cross of gold was presented to the Abyssinian Baptist Church in New York City by Emperor Haile Selassie during his visit. It is of the type which may be used either on a standard or as a processional cross, or on a marble base as an altar cross.

The Hashemite Kingdom of Jordan is rich in lore of Christian iconography, whether one visits the excavations at Mount Nebo overlooking Jordan Valley, or those at Jerash, that elaborate Greco-Roman city founded by veterans from campaigns of Alexander the Great. Crosses at Jerash are seen on uncovered churches built from pagan temples. And at Jerash has been found in the ruins of a primitive fifth-century church at the end of the impressive Street of the

Columns what Dr. John Garstang, excavating for the British School of Archaeology at Jerusalem, has said may be "the earliest sculptured head of Christ," a head as godlike as that of Olympic Zeus, yet eloquent with the agony of atoning suffering which belongs only to the Son of God. This sculptured head, bearded, may date from the second century. If so, it reveals what an artist living in Palestine within a comparatively short time after the death of Christ may have thought his appearance to be. Dr. Garstang believed that the churches at Jerash in Jordan, only fifty-five miles northeast of Jerusalem, perhaps saw the beginnings of Christian architecture, liturgy, and ritual. As we walked among the ruins of Jerash, lovely City of a Thousand Columns in its oasis at the desert's edge, we heard the footsteps of the infant church, moving in and out among temples to Artemis and Jupiter.

One of our Palestine crosses is tinged with childish grotesqueness. It is the Jericho cross from an oasis settlement on the edge of the Judean Wilderness. It began by being a distinctively Russian cross, similar to the eighteenth-century ones having a heart at the center with a tiny cross rising from the heart. But to its arms are attached not only a series of birds, symbolic of the Holy Spirit, but little pendants of red coral and silver sequins. We can imagine it about the neck of a Christian Arab woman of Jericho, on high festival days, when she walked "up to Jerusalem" with furtive glances at every approaching stranger, lest again on this ancient Jericho Road one should "fall among thieves" and be waylaid.

And so, in this Land of the Eternal Cross, we have seen crosses on domes and gables of churches reared by many

7

Beauty of the Byzantine

AFTER STUDYING some of the earliest symbols of the Christian faith in the catacombs of Rome, our quest took us to the East where through the Dark Ages of Europe Byzantine artists developed a mature Christian style.

In Istanbul we became enmeshed in the beauty of the Byzantine symbols, a few specimens of which we subsequently added to our collection of crosses. Here in the domed square churches we saw how Early Christian art had merged into the ornate Byzantine. Here in mosaic, metal, ivory, marble, and stone the symbols of the triumphant royal Redeemer were lifted high until, in 1453, the crescent of onrushing Moslem enthusiasts supplanted the cross and the Osmanli Emperor Mohammed II defeated the last of the Greek Christian emperors, Constantine XIII. The hand-to-hand encounter of the two rulers at the Romanus Gate is a poignant episode in the history of warring man. Yet the tragedy of the battered walls of the Eastern capital had a fructifying effect, for it scattered over Europe scholars and artists who had been sheltered behind their famous landward bulwark.

Mosaic art is one of the distinctive contributions of the Byzantine. One of the most illuminating brief descriptions of what Byzantine mosaic art is, may be found in Peter Meyer's introduction to an elegantly illustrated book, *Byzantine Mosaics*, published by Oxford University Press. According to its author the first prerequisite for making mosaics is availability of an expert glass industry which, by use of mineral salts, produces brilliant colors. Into a foundation of dry masonry very small cubes (tesserae) of glass or colored stone are pressed with a small glass trowel while the plaster is wet. The characteristic gold cubes are made by laying genuine gold leaf on bottle glass. Thus was produced the gleam of Byzantine wall or dome mosaics which is seen in Hagia Sophia, Palermo, Monreale, Ravenna, and Venice—a gleam that lasts a thousand years or more. The fact that the tesserae are set at angles causes them to present their rich colors with a soft and holy light. The stiff unnatural aspect of the figures portrayed is intentional. The enthroned Christ, looking straight at one with wide-eyed, searching love, or Mary holding the Child on her lap in timeless majesty, suggests detachment from all that is earthly and temporal.

The mosaics in the Dome of the Rock in the old Jerusalem Temple Area are probably the work of Byzantine Greeks. Some of the wall mosaics in the Basilica of the Nativity at Bethlehem were fashioned by mosaicists who used leafy Mesopotamian and Persian motifs not usually employed by artists from Constantinople, Greece, and Egypt.

Floor mosaics are made with tesserae of marble or valuable

Cross of Crosses from the author's collection.

Crosses from the Land of the Cross: three Crusader Crosses—center: the
Crusader's or Jerusalem Cross; left and right, excavated from Crusader
tombs, Jerusalem.

Silver cross with pendant Turkish coins, Aleppo. 13th-century (?) cross, China.

Palestinian crosses: Jericho, two Bethlehem, Coptic.

Abyssinian (Ethiopian) crosses: left, from Jerusalem; right, formerly the property of Crown Prince Dessie of Ethiopia, son of Haile Selassie; made of silver coins stamped with head of King Menelik.

Byzantine crosses from Istanbul.

Rugged Balkan crosses: Bulgarian, Herzegovinian, Athenian.

Two Balkan crosses from Dubrovnik, Yugoslavia; at center, a floriated
Greek Cross.

Encolpion, St. George and the Dragon.

Spanish crosses: Burgos, Cordova, Caravaca.

Italian crosses: Rhodes, Bologna, San Marco.

Romanov crosses: Tatiana's, the Tsaritsa's, Romanov anniversary.

Ira W. Martin

Russian icon from Odessa showing Christ
Pantocrator resting his cross on the cloud-
borne world.

Russian crucifix of fine wood overlaid with gold, secured in Russia in 1934. Top, face of the Father with two angels below. On main crossbar, the Virgin, left; St. John, right. Walled and turreted Jerusalem right and left of Christ's feet. Below the suppedaneum, Calvary and skull of Adam.

Russian silver crucifix, 17th or 18th century, associated with Dissenters ("Old Believers") of Russian Church but also in general use among Orthodox. Top, God the Father, with two angels below. At left and right of main crossbar, initials "IC" "XC" meaning "Jesus Christ." Left of body, spear; right, reed with sponge. Below the suppedaneum, skull of Adam. Note: in Byzantine and Greek depictions, and in Western representations antedating 13th century, feet nailed separately, not crossed.

Old cross from Asia Minor.

Lithuanian wayside cross, small flowers blooming beneath shelter.

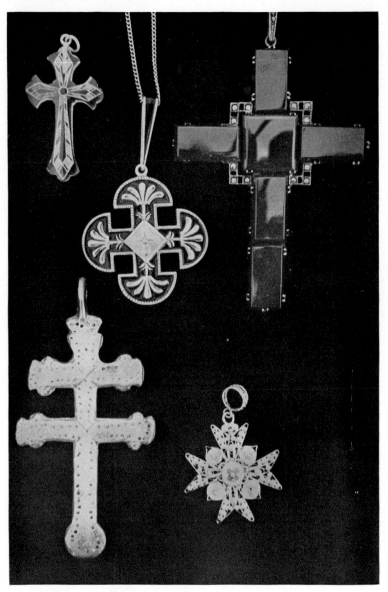

Top: Lithuanian, Norwegian, Swiss. Bottom: American Indian, Madeiran.

Queen Dagmar's Cross, reproduction of one in Copenhagen.

French crosses. Top and bottom: gold, jewel-studded, French Norma style; left: Huguenot Cross, with pendant dove of Holy Spirit; right ivory cross having inside its magnifying glass at center, picture of the youthful Jesus, "Sauveur du monde"

Portuguese National Cross. A cross of this type tops the Jeronymos in Lisbon.

True Maltese Cross of lacelike filigree, arms tapering toward intersection, and having sharp indentations to form cross of eight points.

German crosses. Top: Iron Cross issued in World War II, with date 1939 and swastika; bottom: Iron Cross issued in World War I, showing royal crown and initials of King Frederick William III of Prussia with oak leaves at center and date 1813; left: Hitler's War Mothers' Cross of blue enamel and silver, showing swastika at center and sunburst at intersection; right: garnet cross typical of the Germany of 75 years ago, ends denoting Trinity or fully matured Christian life like a wide-open bud.

English crosses: amethysts in silversmith's art; Canterbury; St. Martin's.

Celtic, "King Arthur's," Iona, Romsey Abbey, Celtic.

Historic and sacred stones assembled by the Reverend J. Lane Miller and formed into a mosaic chancel pavement in the Hanson Place Central Methodist Church, Brooklyn. These stones include ones from Nazareth, Capernaum, Bethlehem, the Jordan, Samaria, Church of the Holy Sepulchre (Jerusalem), Gethsemane, Damascus, Mizpah, Mars Hill (Athens), Golden Gate (Istanbul), Basilica of St. Francis of Assisi, Epworth Rectory (England). The thirty-six stones are in groups of nine each and each carries a legend in tile, indicating place of origin. "I tell you, if these were silent, the very stones would cry out" (Luke 19:40).

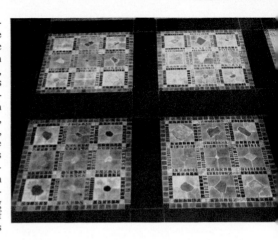

A door of crosses, for records, in the Hanson Place Central Methodist Church, Brooklyn.

American crosses. Top: a fragment once part of Niagara Falls; right, c. 18th-century American Indian work, under missionary influence, Lorraine type; left: modern American Indian, Santa Fé; bottom: cross of malachite, once in collection of Andrew Mellon, Pittsburgh.

Ira W. Ma

An example of altar setting in the Reformed or Free-Church tradition.

The Cross in Splendour. The Reigning Christ, high altar of the Cathedral Church of St. John the Divine, New York.

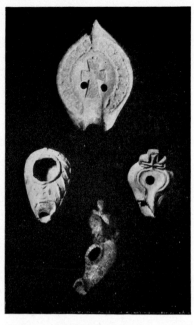

Crosses on lights, ancient clay and metal lamps. Top: clay lamp adorned with cross, 4th-6th century, Carthage, North Africa; bottom: bronze lamp, possibly 6th century, Istanbul; left and right: clay lamps, Near East.

Cross of the Martyrs, Colosseum, Rome.

Young Christian holding his cross aloft. Fr
piece of pottery excavated in the Agora, Athe
Cross dates probably from 5th century.

Loaves, stamped with cross, and fishes (ic
thus), portrayed in floor mosaics of Church
the Multiplying at Tabgha, Galilee, near tra
tional scene of Christ's feeding the multitue
Built possibly in 4th century.

Nimbed Byzantine Christ Pantocrator in dome of Catholicon at Daphni, between Athens and Corinth, Greece.

Prof. Amadeo Maiuri, Superintendent of Antiquities, The Campagna, Naples

Metal "cross" found in 1938 in small room or chapel of house, Casa del Bicentenario, in excavations at Herculaneum (destroyed by eruption of Vesuvius A.D. 79). "Cross" may date 10-12 years before eruption. Possibly originally a bracket for a wall lamp.

Syrian 6th-century silver processional cross with the trisagion inscribed on the front.

The last twelve Mediterranean crosses added to author's collection.

quarried stones much larger than those used in wall and dome mosaics, whose tesserae are usually only a quarter of an inch square. In Istanbul excellent floor mosaics were excavated in 1936 in a terrace of the royal palace area, where we were privileged to see them newly washed and looking as fresh as when they were made in the fourth century. Originally part of the floor of a great hall, they now lie seven feet below the current street level. Their patterns include the figures of a shepherd and horned goats; two ruddy-faced men wrestling; a donkey, lion, and griffon.

In their Christian symbolism Byzantines portrayed a gorgeously attired, triumphant Christ before whose throne adulating emperors prostrated themselves. Thus they taught to humble multitudes the supremacy of Christ. Hagia Sophia, Istanbul, constructed by Justinian at a cost equivalent to fifty million dollars in United States currency, still contains, after centuries of molestation, the greatest series of sacred mosaics in the world. Hagia Sophia is the standard by which other Byzantine art is measured. For hundreds of years its crosses, arches, domes, and half-domes influenced churches in Greece, Cyprus, Russia, the Balkans, and the Middle East, and their influence still continues in modern churches.

When the Moslem conquest claimed Hagia Sophia for a mosque in 1453 the mosaics, the crosses and their Christ were covered with cheap paint and plaster. But now again the Hagia Sophia mosaics have been revealed to modern view by the Byzantine Institute of Boston, under direction of the late Dr. Thomas Whittemore and his successors, with the official encouragement of the Turkish government during the regime of Mustafa Kemel Atatürk and successors.

The uncovering of eight exquisite Byzantine crosses in the

narthex of Hagia Sophia gave a new thrill to all students of
fine arts in religion. As we looked up to these stately symbols with their jeweled terminals of ruby mosaic, we thought
of the historic Christmas in 537 when Justinian the Great
exclaimed upon completion of this vast church, "Thanks be
to God, who has permitted me to accomplish this. Solomon,
I have outrivaled thee!"

For centuries these eight crosses and about one hundred
other crosses with backgrounds of gold mosaics looked down
on Eastern Christendom at worship, for Hagia Sophia was a
capital of the Christian faith in those glowing centuries when
the cross was supreme. Now again the wide-eyed, short-
bearded Byzantine Christ of sixth-century portrayals is
gleaming through. With the whole mosaic scheme of the interior revealed and Christ again leaning in benediction above
the heads of the people, Hagia Sophia is one of the most
impressive structures in the world. Every Christian rejoices
that "he could not be hid."

One of our happiest Byzantine experiences came one morning when we stood with Dr. Whittemore beneath the golden
lunettes of mosaic narrative in Hagia Sophia. In the vestibule
he called our attention to the radiance of the glittering golden
background setting forth in clear blues, reds, and greens the
pleasing pomp of an imperial Mary, enthroned, holding on
her lap a Child carrying a scroll of purple and extending his
young arms in blessing, with Constantine kneeling to offer
them the walls of the city, and Justinian, a model of Hagia
Sophia.

"The glory of these mosaics has never been excelled," said
Dr. Whittemore. "Look at the amazingly soft blue tones of
Mary's gown, the color of deep-blue cornflowers. See how

her apparel is trimmed with meadow-green, laid on bands of gold; notice the sandals of delicate gold outlined with rich red; the cruciferous nimbus of darker red; the delicate emerald greens beneath the throne; the whole background of gleaming gold, and the victorious inscription in Greek."

Then leading us into the narthex he pointed to the Byzantine "Christ-Enthroned" which he had just restored to its original beauty. "The gaze of the Saviour," said Dr. Whittemore, "gives an impression of somewhat languid sad remoteness, conveyed by the face with its wide-open, hazel eyes, its gentle mouth, its oval setting of profuse locks. He is here inviting us into the vast apse. Even during the Moslem use of Hagia Sophia as a mosque, intriguing glimpses of his extended arms peered faintly through the paint. Is it not marvelous how artists whose names we shall never know, introduced these frank, gorgeous colors into liquid glass; and made tiny cubes of gold and silver, covering them with a top layer of glass?"

I have always felt the charm of the substantial Byzantine type of cross—far lovelier than the tall, thin Latin type. The typical Byzantine cross is almost square—although in Hagia Sophia we find also Latin crosses, for in the sixth century the cleavage between Eastern and Western Church had not occurred. The upright of the Byzantine is sometimes slightly longer than the transverse, but the intersection appears near the center of the upright, creating a beautiful balance. Some of its most exquisite forms are on the heavy silver communion plates and chalices for which Byzantine metal workers were noted, the men who in the so-called Dark Ages created the gold altar of Hagia Sophia and the silver iconostasis, even as Cellini wrought his metallic marvels of the Italian Renaissance. The ground plans of typical Byzantine churches, too, trace this cross, surmounted by domes, as the Church of St. Saviour in Istanbul, built by Mary Dukaina to honor martyrs under Diocletian, and adorned by Justinian with resplendent mosaics.

On our desk there stands a thousand-year-old bronze lamp, very small and crudely fashioned, but speaking the intimate workmanship of a pious heart, for its handle is a beautifully proportioned Byzantine cross. It was picked up in Istanbul by a workman excavating between the Blue Mosque of Ahmed and the Sea of Marmara, helping scientists in their search for the Sacred Palace of Byzantine Emperors. This little bronze lamp had lain for centuries, hidden deep under debris of war after war. Evidently someone running from an enemy on a windy night had let it fall while its flame was still burning, for its tiny lid is congealed against the handle. What symbolism in the handle. A cross to lift the light!

A worthy companion piece to the cross-handled lamp is another cross-decorated lamp which Lane bought on his last journey to Mediterranean lands. This rose clay lamp he purchased from the museum in Carthage, ruined city of sacred and secular history in Tunisia, opposite its archenemy, Rome. The lamp, measuring five inches by three, is decorated with a beautifully proportioned Byzantine cross which helps date the piece sometime between the fourth and the sixth centuries. Conventional scrolls surround this cross.

Many Early Christian and Byzantine clay or bronze lamps have a primitive beauty which is appealing. One of the choicest collections we have seen is housed in the Museum of Archaeology in ancient Corinth. There, side by side with pottery running from prehistoric times through the Byzantine, is an amazing group of Greco-Roman lamps arranged in sequence, from the sixth century before Christ when pagan symbols adorned their handles, to Christian times when the cross appeared. In the Metropolitan Museum of Art in New York, also, there is a sequence of Roman and Early Christian crosses and other articles dating from 30 B.C. to A.D. 640 and including the Helen Gould Shepherd collection of terra-cotta lamps. The latter are particularly appealing, representing the piety of poor worshipers who had only the medium of earth to express reverence for the life-bringing cross. We treasure several of these Palestine terra-cotta lamps in our collection, one bearing a stately square cross potent.

Of the three other interesting Byzantine crosses in our collection two are of bronze, probably fashioned between the seventh and the twelfth centuries. One of them is the broken half of a reliquary at whose center is a nimbed cross potent. We wonder who owns the other half of this reliquary? The other has eight round disks extending from its arms, indicative of the eight Beatitudes, or of immortality. The circles are arranged in groups of three, for the Trinity. The third cross, of silver, was found in a musty Turkish bazaar, near the copper stalls. It is overlaid with pleasing blue enamel, with a fragment of ruby-red enamel still showing as background for a simple square cross pommée.

In sacristies of Old World churches there are a few really historic Byzantine crosses. One of the most exquisite is a votive cross of the Eastern emperor, Justinus II, sent to the old St. Peter's Basilica in Rome after sixth-century artists had adorned it with Oriental rubies, sapphires, and pearls and carved it with raised figures and ancient inscriptions.

Its wide transverse arms, extended to the universe, and its upright of almost equal length reaching skyward, are of ultimate beauty. Crude pendants from its transverse are typical of the East. This cross is in the Vatican Museum.

Oval silver forms of panagia or medallions, carved with figures of emperors, saints, or the Christ, are essentially Byzantine. These reliquaries often carry a cross in their decoration.

Leaping like a flame across the blue Mediterranean to Italy, Byzantine art made a rich creative impact upon the West, flowering in the several churches of Ravenna which have survived from the fourth, fifth, and sixth centuries when Ravenna was the capital of the Western Empire. Ravenna antedates Rome as a center of religious art, retaining intact one splendid church after another, jewel boxes of sacred beauty. No wonder Dante welcomed a shelter here in his exile. His tomb today stands in the midst of Early Christian sarcophagi adorned with some of the richest iconographic symbols we have seen anywhere.

In quiet Ravenna, with its citizens flying back and forth to their trades on bicycles, we found a treasure-trove of Early Christian and Byzantine art. We were scarcely prepared for this lavish wealth of iconographic material. Not even Rome itself is so satisfying to people whose avocation is collecting symbols of the Christian faith.

The cloister of San Vitale provides opportunity for studying Byzantine and transitional forms of symbolism. Some of the crosses displayed in that shadowy porch carry the lamb, a symbol which Dr. John S. Thatcher, Director of Dumbarton Oaks Research Library, says was never used on Byzantine crosses after the end of the seventh century. Others carry the blessing hand, which is recognized definitely as a Western type.

We stepped into the amazing interior of Sant' Apollinare Nuovo, the Arian cathedral erected by the good Ostrogoth king, Theodoric the Great, around A.D. 500. The plain red brick exterior of this church which marks the pre-Catholic Italy gives no hint of the two dazzling processions in mosaic extending the entire length of the nave above arches whose pillars bear beautifully proportioned Byzantine crosses. The procession of Blessed Women culminates in the Three Wise Men's presentation of gifts to a rather adult little infant Jesus, sitting on the lap of a very Eastern Mary enthroned like an empress, as in Hagia Sophia. The procession of men saints, with wreaths in hands, approaches an equally imperial *Christos*, enthroned on a cushioned chair with his fine face and chestnut hair and beard accented by a nimbus incorporating a square cross.

The Ravenna cathedral offers its share of iconographic evidence, most of it from the sixth century, in the famous bronze cross at the right of the altar, the silver cross of Bishop Agnellus, and the pulpit or reading desk, nicknamed "the throne of Arian bishops," which rises above a screen carved with what we call a primer of Christian symbolism. It carries six lambs in the top row; then six peacocks for immortality; then a row of six antelopes, typifying young converts enjoying solitude and drinking the water of life as a hart drinks at the waterbrooks. Below is a row of six doves; with six ducks and six varieties of ichthus on the lowest rows near the floor.

Adjacent to the cathedral is the fifth-century Baptistry converted from a Roman bath to a Christian chapel, a treasure of mosaics made about A.D. 450 and displaying a Roman vitality in the portrayal of the prophets, in contrast to the rigid figures in the Hagia Sophia mosaics. Most remarkable is the depiction in the dome, above a polygonal font large enough for immersion, of the baptism of Jesus whose body shows through the transparency of the water in "rippling" mosaics. No finer mosaics exist in the world than these, the oldest and best in Ravenna. They come from the same early period which has likewise given Ravenna the marvelous beauty of the so-called Mausoleum of Galla Placidia, the fair Empress and devout Christian matron who, coming from Constantinople as regent for her young brother Honorius, son of the Eastern Emperor Theodosius, erected a noble church in gratitude for her safe arrival. Taken later as wife of the barbarian Ataulphus who carried her off to Gaul, Placidia returned to Ravenna and founded about A.D. 440 the fine little structure. It is in the form of an almost square cross, lined with mosaics. The dome is of dark blue mosaics, spangled with golden stars giving background to a Latin cross surrounded by symbols of the four Evangelists. This large cross is one of the first ever incorporated into a monumental structure. Over the massive sarcophagus of the Empress, large enough to contain her body seated on a cypress throne and resembling an altar facing one as he enters, is a cross-bearing figure of the Saviour. At the opposite end is a lunette depicting a charming young Jesus as a happy shepherd, like David, surrounded by his faithfully tended sheep, one of which he is feeding. On top of the red-tiled roof is not a cross but an acorn, symbol of strength and eternal life. The acorn rests also on top of the "tomb of Dante" not far away.

In the Church of San Vitale, built in A.D. 525 when Justinian was repulsing King Theodoric, there is a portrayal of Justinian's wife the Empress Theodora and her court in the gleaming Persian brocades and jeweled crowns and necklaces of that extravagant period. The mosaics in the hem of her garment reproduced the Three Magi of the façade of Bethlehem Basilica.

Though small, San Vitale reminded us at once of the interior of Hagia Sophia with its central apse under a noble dome, its many arches resting on sculptured capitals. Yet actually it preceded Hagia Sophia (dedicated in 537) and was suggested by churches in Thessalonica, with its ground plan based on a Christian baptistry. Many of the mosaics encrusting the walls are composed of such small tesserae that they look like woven tapestry rather than glass and marble cubes. Artists were imported from Constantinople to adorn the sacred walls and to train Western workers.

Further enrichment of our understanding of Early Christian symbols we found when, driving three miles toward the sea, we came to Sant' Apollinare in Classe, ancient naval base of imperial Rome. Here are massive stone sarcophagi of notables who lived in the fifth, sixth, and eighth centuries at Ravenna. These tombs display some of the finest series of Christian symbolism in the world. Lambs carrying crosses; peacocks symbolic of renewed life; the Chi Rho; the date palm of victorious martyrdom; sacred birds of the spirit; vines with interwoven branches; the serpents of wisdom; tree of life; lions indicative of Jesus as the Lion of the Tribe of Judah; St. John's four rivers of life—all are here. One of the finest, with its Byzantine crosses and elegant peacocks among fruitful grapevines, is that of the seventh-century Archbishop Theodore. And in the half-dome of the apse above a flowery meadow where the sheep (apostles) graze, is a tremendous mosaic cross resting on a ground spangled with golden stars and jewels.

About a hundred years before the Ravenna artists were adorning their fifth-century churches other mosaic workers in a little basilica along the murmuring Sea of Galilee were pressing into place mosaics which were recovered in 1932 from under the sand where they had lain since the Persian invasion of 614, or some other destructive incursion. There at Tabgha, on a supposed site of Christ's miraculous feeding of the multitude, a portion of floor and apse has been scientifically cleaned and protected by the erection of a simple basilica over these rare gems of iconographic art. We were delighted to see lively depictions of the animals and flowers of the marshland along the Sea which Jesus loved—herons, geese, flamingos, reeds, lilies, and lotus. And in the apse beyond the altar, the most famous mosaic fragment, a tall basket containing five round flat loaves of Syrian bread, each bearing a small square cross. On each side of the symbolic basket is a fish standing on its tail. Thus at the eastern end of the Mediterranean, the same symbols were being used as in the catacombs of Rome at about the same period.

Other gleaming crosses we found built into the mosaics of the famous Church of Daphne, along the Sacred Way west from Athens to Eleusis and Corinth. The iconography of Daphne ranks high in the history of sacred mosaics. A more beautiful portrayal of Christ triumphant we saw in the extensive eleventh-century Daphne wall mosaics—for Byzantines abhorred empty spaces and filled every available nook with figures or conventional designs. Here we saw Jesus riding into Jerusalem on a young colt. His garments are a rich dull green. Rose robes have been placed under him on the docile colt, with other colorful garments strewn under his feet by children. Jerusalem's walls loom in mellow ivory against a background of gold mosaics. Around the head of Jesus is a nimbus incorporating a square Greek cross. Byzantine crosses are carved on fallen fragments in this quaint monastery church—small in size, as are most Byzantine churches, because congregations stand to worship.

A beautifully proportioned Byzantine cross which Lane bought in Istanbul suggests how the same motifs and proportions in crosses extended from one end of the Mediterranean to the other. This cross, three inches long, whose upright is only slightly longer than its transverse arm, is evidently about nine hundred years old—which places it within the Byzantine period. Each of its ends is decorated with three little circular disks, accenting the Trinity.

Byzantine thought contributed much to Russian and Balkan iconography and architecture. So while a dark age was shadowing Europe and sixth-century barbarians were rampant; and later when ninth-century Saracens were raiding Rome, Byzantine religious art was being produced with splendid artistic and religious effect in new areas.

Thus the cross can be traced from its Eastern infancy to its Western maturity in the Mediterranean. The cross of Christ leaps over barriers of sea and mountain, links centuries and civilizations by the certainty of its life-giving power.

⊰ 8 ⊱

Russian Crosses

THE CHRISTIAN cross entered Russia largely through the missionary work of the Greek Church at Constantinople. As early as 987 Vladimir, prince of Kiev, became a Christian and introduced the faith into Kievan Russia. More than nine centuries later following the establishment of the Union of Soviet Socialist Republics and in spite of freedom of worship provided by the constitution, the cross went underground in most parts of the land.

Traveling in the Crimea in 1933–35, we found torgsins, or shops which had been set up for foreigners, heavily stocked with Russian crosses and handsome liturgical equipment at prices so low that they revealed the disregard in which these treasures were locally held. It was then that we secured for our collection numerous superb Russian crosses.

Usually they were lying in cases with a background of gorgeous, cross-emblazoned brocaded copes and velvet chasubles, formerly used in Russian imperial chapels and local churches. These vestments, remarkable examples of the art of hand-looming, were being bargained for and divided among merchants seeking fabrics for evening wraps and ladies' purses.

The most historic of our Russian crosses is an enameled Romanov cross struck in 1913 to commemorate the three hundredth anniversary of the founding of the Romanov dynasty—that line of sometimes corrupt, but often able rulers. Among them was Peter the Great, founder of St. Petersburg, modernizer of the old Oriental Russia, who pushed through to the Baltic where he gained a commercial foothold. It was he who first brought the Orthodox Church under direct control of the government, a policy of questionable wisdom in any age.

All iconographers are grateful to the Romanov dynasty, which was designing beautiful crosses in Russia while the Pilgrim Fathers were pushing into the New World with bold Christian faith, but little interest in aesthetics of worship.

Our Romanov cross is fashioned after the design worked out by Michael Feodorovitch in 1913 for the last of the Romanov czars, the mystical, fatalistic Nicholas II, during the three hundredth anniversary celebration. The reverse side of this cross bears the ironical inscription, "May God give our Czar a long reign. 1613–1913." Five years later the Russian imperial family was liquidated. The obverse side of the Romanov cross is of white, red, and green enamel on which is outlined another simple Russian cross with the three characteristic transverse bars. The top one stands for the titleboard on which Pilate wrote, more truly than he knew, "This is Jesus, the King of the Jews." The wider bar is the one to which the Saviour's arms were nailed. And the short oblique support or suppedaneum is the bar to which his feet were affixed. A beautiful circle of immortality surrounding the intersection of the main crossbar with the upright is decorated with two series of twelve dots in groups of three, indicative of Christ's Twelve Men and the Trinity. The Romanov cross is crowned with a high pointed cap, resembling both an Oriental turban lined with red and the dome of the characteristic Russian church. Resting on top of the royal cap is a simple square cross.

In addition to our Romanov cross, we treasure two crosses which belonged to members of the imperial family. One of them is a fine Greek silver cross from the personal belongings of the last czarina, Alexandra Feodorovna. The outlines of this Russian cross, dating from about 1750, imposed on a simple Western cross, are traced on a base of silver bearing inscriptions in the old Slavonic language of ancient Russia, and the "IC–XC" ("Jesus Christ"). The reverse bears a familiar prayer used in daily ritual and as an Eastern anthem: "God will rise; His enemies will scatter; after beholding His face all-glorious and awesome they will run from His presence. God, keep evil away from the wearer of this cross."

The other cross, which lies side by side with the czarina's cross in our cabinet, is a more highly treasured one from the personal collection of her daughter, Grand Duchess Tatiana. This cross dates from the seventeenth century. Fragments of delicate green and blue enamel still adorn this fine piece of Russian art and set off the inner cross which rises out of a heart and rests upon a crown of thorns. Rising parallel to the upright of the cross are a tall spear and a rod bearing the sponge, reminding us of the merciful incident in the Crucifixion of Jesus, when "one of them at once ran and took a sponge, filled it with vinegar, and put it on a reed, and gave it to him to drink. . . . And Jesus cried again with a loud voice and yielded up his spirit" (Matt. 27:48, 50).

A larger and more beautifully enameled cross of the same period we found one day in a torgsin at Odessa. It, too, has an inner cross rising from a heart above the skull and crossbones, denoting the conquered sin of the original Adam, on whose skull the atoning blood drops of Jesus fall. The ends of the cross swell out into beautiful forms suggesting the domes of Russian churches.

No collection of Russian crosses would be complete without at least one icon or image. Although Greece and the Balkans have produced many historic icons, no land has specialized in this form of religious art more than Russia. Her Oriental love of the ornate led monk-craftsmen in remote monasteries to produce extremely elaborate icons; toiling lovingly, they painted on wood, representations of Christ, of the Madonna, of favorite Russian saints—Nicholas, Dmitri, Peter, Ivan, and Alexis. Secular artists, too, formed schools famous for their icons in Novgorod, Moscow, Pskov, and various smaller towns.

When the spoliation of churches occurred in Soviet Russia, it threw out of employment families of artists who for generations had been making icons, following Greco-Byzantine designs, with inspiration also from Persia. The village of Palekh, two hundred miles east of Moscow, noted for centuries for its painted icons, resorted to making lacquered boxes on which the craftsmen now depict secular subjects, flowery fields, folk tales about sacks of buried rubles, or border designs in flowing gold, based on Persian patterns.

The last of the Romanov czars had a famous collection of icons in the Alexandrovsky Palace at Czárskoe Seló, dating from the fifteenth century and revealing the richest forms of Russian ornamentation. Even in the bathroom of his palace at sunny Yalta he kept an icon hanging; also a many-headed Hydra, familiar to Orthodox Christians as a symbol of the prolific nature of sin and heresy.

Quite as impressive as the czar's ornate icon are the simpler ones which hung in rural churches and peasant homes— simple wooden panels about which the worship life of the family centered. For the icon was the most universal expression of the religious life of the Russian people before the Revolution.

The icon now in our own collection was bought by Lane in a torgsin at Odessa, 1934. We shall never know from what Crimean church it had been carried. Its old wooden panel bears a very simple, moving portrait of the Saviour, a slender, refined, sensitive face framed with soft chestnut locks parted in the middle above a high forehead. The short pointed beard, delicate mouth, slender nose, and large deep-set brown eyes suggest a living, kindly Man, the Son of God, who once moved with stately power among the people. That beautiful olive countenance, so free from the stereotyped rigidity of Byzantine types, stirs us by its noble simplicity as it hangs on the wall of our living room beside a Persian prayer rug. This beautiful face is framed in a simple overlay of brass, whose design drapes the shoulders of Jesus with the soft folds of a toga and shows him carrying in his arms the cloud-lifted world surmounted by a simple cross, the cross of his redeeming love for mankind. The only elaborate feature of our icon is the sunburst of brass and brilliants which forms a crownlike nimbus or "glory" for this two-hundred-year-old symbol out of the religious heart of old imperial Russia.

Icons may have been made first in Byzantium in the eleventh century. This form of liturgical art is characteristic of most of the Orthodox churches in Russia, Greece, Rumania, and Bulgaria. The screen (iconostasis, sometimes iconostas) which separates nave from sanctuary is often richly decorated with icons. In some Russian churches the iconostasis is many tiered, having one row of icons above the other as on the façade of the Metropolitan Church of Rumania in Bucharest, built in the sixteenth century.

The fifth of our Russian crosses associated with the former aristocracy is an elegant gold one from the collection of the Princess Chardrinos in Moscow. It derives from one of the many hoards of personal treasures thrust upon the markets of the world—in this case Madison Avenue, New York—by aristocrats exiled subsequent to 1918. It is not of the orthodox Russian type, but a well-proportioned Latin cross with graceful trefoil ends, its surface embellished with delicately etched flowers. At times it looks like a bit of fine old lace, again like an Armenian pattern with Persian influences. It avoids all figure portrayals of the Christ, carries no inscription, no sacred monogram. The most distinguishing detail is a six-pointed golden star at the center of the circle of immortality which bounds the intersection of the arms. And at the center of the star, forever reminding us of the quest of the Magi who followed its heavenly original from fields afar, a rose is blooming.

The story of the Christianizing of Slav Russia is fraught with lively dramatic details. Late in the tenth century there was born a son who became Vladimir, grand duke and founder of Kiev, present capital of the Russian Ukraine. This polygamous pagan warrior, who conquered city after city in Galicia, sailed down Russian rivers to conquer Bulgaria, erected new heathen shrines, and put to death people who were already practicing Christianity in secret. Following a suggestion from his court advisers, in 987 he sent delegations to look into the religions of the nations surrounding him. An old chronicle tells how these men brought back an adverse report from the Moslem Bulgarians along the Volga River, "because they found in them no spirit of joy," but only "sorrow and a great stench." The heavy temples of the Germanic tribes left them cold, because they found no beauty there. But when they stood beneath the miraculous dome of Hagia Sophia at Constantinople, capital of Byzantine Christianity, they were spellbound by its architecture and its service of worship, participated in by ten bishops, eight hundred priests, a choir of two hundred men and women and two hundred boys, with an orchestra of three hundred playing harps, mandolins, zithers, and dulcimers. The whole impression so thrilled the emissaries from pagan Russia that Vladimir desired baptism into a faith that could produce such heavenly beauty. So at Kherson in the Crimea, not far from the Yalta church we were to visit later, Vladimir was baptized and an immediate baptism of his people followed.

The Byzantine Christian symbolism of the golden age which spread from the Bosporus up to the Dnieper a thousand years ago is still seen in Kiev's Sophia Cathedral with its amazingly preserved mosaics and elegant architecture, combining features of Syrian, Byzantine, Persian, and Roman influences. And in the Kiev-Pechersk Monastery, which has been allowed to remain unmarred, is an outstanding example of Middle Age Slavonic architecture.

From the point of view of craftsmanship, the finest of our Russian crosses is a slender wooden crucifix about twelve inches long, of fine smooth wood, overlaid with plaster on which the painted design is applied. This perfect specimen of Russian Orthodox cross with its two parallel bars, denoting Christ's ministry to Gentiles and Jews, and the oblique bar to which his feet were nailed, is overlaid with solid gold leaf whose rich tones have grown more mellow with the centuries. Superimposed on the gold background, a simple wooden cross is painted, and to it is affixed a slender, crucified Jesus, nimbed with a golden aureole, bearing on its square cross the Russian letters for Alpha and Omega. Right and left of this "inhabited" cross are portrayals of the weeping mother and the sympathizing friend, John, while above the titleboard rises from a bank of clouds the conventional portrayal of the Father with arms extended in benediction, and above this a dove denoting the third Person of the Trinity and two well-wrought cherubim kneeling in adoration.

A distinctive feature of this valuable crucifix is the representation of medieval Jerusalem on the oblique suppedaneum. The city walls and romantic towers show the interest of the artist in the architecture of the Middle Ages. They lift the whole design above the depressing, rocky Calvary on which the cross is seen to rest, a skull depicting Golgotha and death.

One of our most appreciated Russian crosses is the simplest imaginable. Just a hand-carved piece of olive wood which grew on the sunny slopes of the Crimea. It was carved into an Eastern cross with trefoil ends by an old man whom we saw one day sitting in the portico of an elaborately domed church in beautiful cypress-trimmed Yalta on the Black

Sea. The door ajar suggested that here was a place still used
for the worship of God, so we walked through its once-lovely
garden, whose broken palm trees and weedy rosebushes
and rain-strewn gravel paths looked as if no one had ex-
pended money or care upon them since they were last
groomed for the summer visit by the family of the Czar. At
the half-open door sat an old man with a broad Slavic face,
pockmarked, and heavily bearded. He was mending shoes,
trying to get one whole pair out of three. Seeing our interest,
he asked in a kindly tone, "Amerikanski?"

Upon our nod of assent, he rose and escorted us inside the
church. He was its priest. Ragged and impoverished, he still
tended the fires of faith. His cot was here, for he had no
other home. Nothing had been changed from former days.
Elaborate brass-framed icons were intact. On one altar, near
a painting of St. Nicholas, patron of Czar Nicholas II, was a
vase of fresh Crimean flowers. The red carpet was badly
stained by candle grease. Panes of glass were missing. But if
there had been no money for repairs, at least there had been
no desecration. People still could come here to pray.

We were about to leave when we saw near the door of the
church, for sale among tall wax tapers, one little hand-carved
trefoil cross of olive wood. The tragic, hungry Yalta priest
accepted our American *valuta* as eagerly as we accepted the
new-found treasure.

The situation of this priest and his neglected church
summed up for us the present state of the church in the
U.S.S.R. Hostility to religion was proclaimed from the beginning of the regime, when party members were required to
renounce their faith. Many Russian Orthodox churches which

had been heavily subsidized by the government were deprived of their state revenues and shorn of participation in the registration of marriages, births, and deaths.

Other Russian crosses of considerable age enrich our collection. A silver one of the Western type is carved with the Eastern three-barred cross, set amid prayers written in Russian, pleasingly ornamented with spear points at its center and stout round knobs of silver at every available point. Another has been so long used for worship that the ring from which it was suspended is worn entirely through. Still another, a square cross of deep blue Russian enamel, is outlined against a floriated background of brilliants, studded with a ruby-red stone and four large sapphire blue ones, clearly a badge of honor with which some forgotten hero was decorated. In contrast to this flamboyant cross is an exquisitely simple one, cut from a single piece of flawless, cold Russian crystal, which was once a fragment of some glistening mountain recess in a land rich in untapped minerals.

In heavy contrast to the delicacy of this cross is a green-brown bronze one of which its seller could tell us nothing, except that "it was for long underground." Its price led us to believe that it is older than our silver ones. At its center is carved the robed figure of St. Nicholas surrounded by four colleagues, a good example of the "inhabited" cross. This may date from the sixteen hundreds or earlier.

It is not surprising that our Palestine Jericho cross has a Russian cross as the basis of its design, for in Palestine the Russian Church, prior to World War I, had large holdings dating from the time of Nicholas I. In 1852 he secured from the Ottoman government at Constantinople the privilege of "protecting" the rights of Orthodox Christians in the Holy Places. Through a trivial argument over the custody of fifteen silver lamps kept burning by Latins, Orthodox, and Armenians near the traditional birthplace of Jesus, trouble broke out between the Russians and the French who a century earlier had been assigned to protect all Christians visiting the Holy Land. England was inevitably drawn into the contest of power politics and the Crimean War was under way in 1854. The question of worship privileges in the Holy Land became submerged under the struggle between England, France, and Turkey who combined against Russia in a contest for the Danubian principalities; control of the strategic Dardanelles; the admission of Turkey to the family of European powers; and the prevention of Russia's gaining Constantinople, and control of the route to India.

The humbling of Nicholas I at Sevastopol was a dark day for the Romanov dynasty. But from the bloody Crimean struggle there emerged a glorious heroine, Florence Nightingale, who in the vermin-infested barracks at Scutari opposite Constantinople, with her staff of forty English nurses, founded the modern profession of healers of broken men and women. The Red Cross, with the square ruby-colored emblem of life-giving compassion emblazoned on a pure white ground, grew out of this ministry of mercy. The red cross is truly a descendant of the redemptive cross of the Great Physician who healed by Galilee.

The last accession to our Russian group was found in New York's lower East Side. It is of heavy silver and measures three and one-half inches in length. Markings on the reverse side of this triple-barred cross indicate "of pure silver." It carries the date 1722 but its fashioning may be earlier for varied markings on the back have been made by several hands, in several periods. Some are finely engraved, as the one which is translated "St. Petersburg," below which is the imperial crown with a small cross rising from it. Below this crown are initials which may stand for Peter I. Below this are two crudely-pricked initials, looking like the English "X.B." and standing for "Christ is risen." Then, in similarly crude pricks, "1722 6/31."

The obverse of this Russian cross depicts the usual Russian crucified Lord, with arms extended wide, and feet not crossed on the suppedaneum. Below the latter there is something which looks like an effort to portray the tomb of Adam, associated by tradition with Calvary in Jerusalem. Christ is nimbed with a circular aureole. Two well-carved cherubim reach down from above the Saviour's head to help him. On a fourth crossbar above the cherubim is a nimbed head which symbolizes the glorified Redeemer. Around the widest arm of the cross are words of what is apparently a Russian hymn of the Resurrection.

This type of Russian cross, with its eight extremities, is especially associated with the Raskolniks, or dissenters in the Russian Church. But it is also used by the Orthodox.

✄ 9 ✄

Rugged Balkan and
Baltic Crosses

BALKAN CROSSES are eloquent of the robust, colorful qualities of the people of many races and shades of belief who inhabit the pivotal peninsula jutting out from southeastern Europe into the Adriatic, Black, and Aegean Seas.

There is a stolid, substantial beauty about Balkan crosses which suggests the mighty mountains and rushing rivers which water the sunny valleys of vines, roses, and grain tended by people whose boundary lines have been fluctuating ever since the days of Philip of Macedon. The Rhodope and the Balkan Mountains of Bulgaria gave their name to the entire section comprising Greece, Yugoslavia, Bulgaria, and Rumania; the Carpathians and Transylvanian Alps of Rumania, the Grammas summits of old Serbia; the detached and purpler "god-inhabited" mountains of Greece. These ranges induced isolation of the sturdy people living there and led them to develop forms of religious art as diversified as their modes of political thought.

The Balkans have long been on the route of those who advanced to conquest, uprooting contented tillers of the earth and builders of noble cities. Greeks, Romans, Byzantine emperors; wild tribes of Avars and Huns out of the steppes of central Europe; Russians, Turks—all levied their toll on life. Therefore, the iconography of the Balkans is particularly diversified, but is consistently marked by sincere integrity of hand-wrought design.

The crosses and icons found in ancient monasteries on peaks of mountain fastnesses are as pleasing to behold as peasant crosses for sale in towns. The picturesque peasant art ways of Balkan people present contrasts to the surprising modernity of some of their cities.

We are fortunate to have secured our Balkan crosses before the Iron Curtain of isolation shut off some of the lands of their origin. The two Greek crosses which became the foundation of our collection have already been described.

In the silversmiths' shops of modern Athens we found many heavy silver crosses on chains, some of which had been brought as gifts to the staff of the Metropolitan of Athens by pilgrims from other lands where the Greek Orthodox Church flourishes. Needing ready cash, the recipients had placed them on the market.

One cross bears on its ancient filigree foundation the same conventional cabochons and diamond shapes which decorate our Armenian cross from Jerusalem. It has no figure of Christ or saints, but a floriated crown studded with a green stone glorifying the Saviour's crown of thorns. Its significant feature is a group of old Turkish coins pendant from its three arms. These coins from Ottoman Turkey are not only decorative, but they are also a parable of the power which flows with energizing effect when money is brought in contact with the sacrificial cross of Christ.

Another Greek cross appears to have come from the island of Crete—home of superb Aegean art in the Minoan period four thousand years ago. This is an inexpensive metal cross a few generations old. It has the same intersecting spear points and blue, red, and green gems as our first Athenian cross. But instead of having tiny pendant crosses or coins hanging from its arms, it has wheel-shaped disks in which we see the symbolism of the onsweeping progress of the Kingdom of God when given impetus by believers.

Two simple filigree crosses of the square Greek variety secured in energetic modern Corinth, are links with the ministry of Paul, who preached "Christ crucified, a stumbling-block to Jews and folly to Gentiles, but to those who are called, both Jews and Greeks, Christ the power of God and the wisdom of God" (I Cor. 1:23 f.).

The last three of our Greek crosses were found by Lane on his final visit to the shop where the whole collection had begun so unexpectedly many years earlier. Sauntering again into the narrow street where he hoped to find the shop surviving a second World War and guerilla disorders, he was delighted to find not only the same tiny store, but also Mr. Philip, hale and hearty, offering objects of religious art to American collectors. Mr. Philip recognized Lane and brought out from his cabinet what became our three final Greek accessions. One was of fine silver filigree, gold-dipped, and studded with cheerful red and green gems. It had originated in Euboea, the long, slender island which sprawls in Aegean sunshine—a natural 100-mile breakwater protecting Athens,

Corinth, Megara—a region anciently famous for its chestnuts and its fine horses—possibly the secret of the success of Attica's "thousand horsemen." As long as Athens had Euboea for her ally, she safeguarded not only her own capital, but the north Aegean lanes of wind-blown wheat triremes on whose safe arrival Byzantium depended. Demosthenes rated Athens' control of Euboea as essential.

So our cheerful Euboea cross reflects the warm spring rain and the south wind which fostered the grain. In its ruby-red stone we see reminders of the crystalline rocks that crop out in the southern part of the island, and of fine Euboean marbles, capable of high polish, which found their way into the hands of Greek sculptors. The red stones also reminded us that one Euboean town was noted for its murex shells which, like those of ancient Tyre, were exported to dye rich wool stuffs with their deep red-purplish hue.

The second of these three crosses came from mountainous Thessaly, today part of Yugoslav territory. Its equal arms are pierced by spear points, its center adorned by a bright red stone. From its lower arms, coins dangle. This cross of Thessaly was designed not far from Mount Olympus on the border of Macedonia to which region Paul first carried the Christian gospel into Europe.

The third cross had originated in Macedonia, hence another association with Paul. This one hundred and fifty year old symbol consists of a gracefully shaped silver-gilt, carved background for the form of a crucified Jesus, whose uplifted arms and limbs are elongated and whose head wears a nimbus of glory.

Our most substantial-looking Balkan crosses are from the Dalmatian coastal strip of Yugoslavia, where the luxuriant

mountains drop sheer to the Adriatic and leave a succession
of colorful towns whose Christian faith dates from the second century. The Dalmatian city of Split, the ancient Spalato
or Salona, was the birthplace and also the last residence of
the tyrant Diocletian (A.D. 284–305), who persecuted the
early Christians because in their community he saw a rival
to his authority at Rome. Some of the ruins of the despot's
royal buildings are foundations of Yugoslav churches today.
The settlement of Dubrovnik (Ragusa) by mixed groups of
Illyrians, Latins, Slavs, and Greeks in the seventh century
provided their Christian religion with a mixture of symbols.
Today in that city there is at times open conflict between
Eastern and Western bodies of Christendom. However, the
chief influence is Latin. The one long principal street, the
Stradone, is dominated at the west end by the Franciscan
Monastery with its "oldest pharmacy in Europe," and at its
east end by the Dominican Monastery. Neither of these Western churches, nor the unattractive baroque Gospa (Cathedral) or the Church of the patron saint, Blaise, reveals anything of the typical Balkan architecture we have seen in the
Byzantine churches of Rumania and Bulgaria.

There are as many varieties of peasant crosses in Ragusa
as there are headgears in the picturesque market place.
Many of them are treasured heirlooms. Two which we secured are possibly a hundred years old. The smaller is of silver, studded with red and blue and green stones suggestive
of the gay peasant embroideries on Balkan jackets and
dresses. It has dangling pendants similar to the Coptic ostrich eggs and is marked by a beauty of tapering line toward
its center. The larger cross, whose silver has been gilded by
a rich tint of yellow gold, shows a stubbiness of proportion

as substantial as that of the white-kerchiefed peasants we watched selling red leather belts, baby dresses, chickens, and melons in the market. Its surface is delicately embossed with conventionalized leaves of life and other Persian details. There is no figure of Christ but through open carved work at the center of the cross peers a coin on the obverse of which are Mary and the Child and on the reverse, the crucified Lord. Its maker, like the Armenians, disliked pictorial representations. Remembering the words of the aged John, "Little children, keep yourselves from idols," they clung to the formal scroll and vine.

Our most beautiful Yugoslav cross is almost square, its arms tapering toward the center with the corners skillfully filled in by four spear points worked into the design of a circle or crown. The refined filigree tracery of scrolls and tiny diagonal figures, the flower at its center, adorned with a ruby-red jewel contrasting with its other jewels of Byzantine blue and green, give it a distinct kinship to the Persian influence of the Middle East. This lovely Yugoslav cross, almost three inches square, had drifted into a dark little shop tucked in among bazaars specializing in gay leather bags and red slippers. It came from the Herzegovinian town of Mostar on the Neretva River, which enters the Adriatic at Dubrovnik. We were glad that some circumstance floated this squatty, substantial peasant cross down the ancient waterway.

We always admired, also, our two elaborate specimens which express Slavic piety in fine-spun filigree, studded with silver beadwork and small cabochons. One of these crosses, bearing no figures, has at its center a hinged amulet in the form of a Latin cross, lined with bright red cloth peering from under filigree. The other cross, incorporating a Latin depiction of the crucified Jesus between spear points, appears to be from Herzegovina, a Dalmatian region snuggling on the south shore of the fjord Boka Kotorska, where its small homes set amid pencil cypresses look as if the encroaching Black Mountains of Montenegro would push them into the quiet waters of the bay.

Once in Dubrovnik, we came upon an irresistible little solid gold cross whose owner parted with it for just the price of its high-karat yellow gold. He cared little for the finely wrought work of its designer who had carved at the four ends of this loveliest of our Ragusan crosses four delicate scallop shells, symbols of the religious pilgrim. We had long wanted a cross decorated with the pilgrim shell and here it was, bought in the town where Richard the Lionhearted had been shipwrecked en route home from the Holy Lands. Scallop shell was used in Early Christian symbolism to indicate James the Greater, brother of Jesus, who many a time along the shores of the Sea of Galilee had taken up dripping shells in his nets along with fish. The shell was later used on the cloak, armor, or pennons of those who had been pilgrims to the land of the Fisherman of souls. Sometimes an actual scallop shell was stuck in the hat of the pilgrim returning home joyful that at last his vows were fulfilled. The shell, used sometimes by early Christians to scoop up water for baptism, became a Christian symbol for that rite.

The last of our Yugoslav crosses was acquired by Lane on his final journey East. Arriving on the first cruise ship to enter the old Dubrovnik harbor after World War II, he found the Stradone shops unbelievably depleted. Yet he discovered one silver symbol unsurpassed by any other in our large group of Balkan crosses. It is composed of six round, buttonlike, silver medallions of filigree having highly polished centers, and shows relationship to several other of our Yugoslav crosses although it is unlike any of them. Its form identifies it with the West, and its proportions are stately—three and one-half inches by two and one-half. This Balkan cross holds its own "above the wrecks of time."

Of Rumanian crosses, we have only one type, a small one of blue enamel on silver, carrying on its trefoil ends the letters "IC–XC" ("Jesus Christ"). It still bears the ribbon of Rumanian national colors, red, yellow, blue, by which it was hanging on the shopkeeper's wall.

This simple Balkan cross suggests the elaborate icons we saw on a visit to the Cotroceni Palace of Queen Marie in Bucharest. This remarkable woman had her private sitting room done in the style of a peasant cottage, using textiles and ceramics she did so much to revive for the benefit of her people after World War I. As we looked at the icons beside her couch, and at the small Greek cross beside her bed, we remembered that her mother was a Russian Grand Duchess and that Marie came by her taste for crosses quite naturally, even though she was also a granddaughter of Queen Victoria. She visited Moscow often as a child and remembered those occasions when, in maturity, she contemplated the Russian crucifix which we saw by her tremendous fireplace in the royal palace.

The most prevalent cross we saw in the Rumanian churches, which are similar in style to round-arched Orthodox churches of Russia and Greece with their "crinkled" cupolas, is a square cross-crosslet. In fact, the one on the palace of the Metropolitan of Bucharest has its intersecting arms crossed and recrossed so many times that it looks like an aggregation of plus signs. The cross-crosslet tops the amazing wooden steeple of the famous wooden church of Maramuresh with its double roofs beetling down like mountain avalanches over its low first story. So, too, the cross-crosslet tops the polygonal cupolas of the stately little Byzantine Mitropolia or Episcopia, the state church adjacent to the Chamber of Deputies, scene of state ceremonies of worship.

This head church of the Rumanian people is so adorned without and within that it is really an elaborate jewel box. Its crosses spring from the crescent moon, a symbol of Mary, found under many Russian crosses, with chains swinging from the crossbars. Its façade is a feast for the iconographer, for it is paved with a series of painted icons in rows; and its front portico carries a fresco, quaintly showing a small weeping Judas sitting on the arm of Satan, who clutches the moneybag behind Judas' back so that he cannot see it. Here is the iconography of greed.

In simple Rumanian village churches, and in city churches, in among all her diversified peoples, the cross of Rumania is everywhere. Bessarabians weave it into their carpets; Transylvanians put their icon of St. George on glass; Oltenians weave it into their aprons and napkins embroidered in wool and gold. The poorest peasant or the most cultured Rumanian physician adorns his walls with icons and crosses. Although modern Rumania boasts Roman ancestry, her soul looks toward the East and draws its art from Byzantium.

Rumania, before its Russian domination, had an independent state church. Its head, attired in the long black robes, high hat, and flowing veil, was a personage of dignity and honor, wearing on his breast crosses of various types given him by admirers among the fourteen million of Rumania's population of eighteen million who are baptized adherents of his faith.

As in Lithuania, the wayside wooden crosses or *prie-dieus* of Rumania reveal originality and sincere beauty. Devout peasants, who before the Iron Curtain closed in on land and people owned 90 per cent of the land and comprised 80 per cent of the people, tilled rich wheat fields coveted by hungry western neighbors. They placed wooden shrines at crossroads, or in the midst of their fields, flocks, or near their whitewashed thatched cottages where they spent the long winter evenings carving while their wives embroidered or spun or wove.

One day while we were strolling through the little main square of the Rumanian oil port of Constanza on the Black Sea, we were attracted by an outdoor exhibit of oil paintings by Rumanian artists. The one to which we fell victim and purchased, we call our "Rumanian Angelus," for against the spring sky which has just watered the sowed fields, a wayside cross is shown, with a little pointed roof protecting its painting of the crucifixion. Close by is an icon of Mary. Beside these symbols which express his faith for the life-giving harvests, a smock-clad, sturdy Rumanian farmer stands absorbed in prayer. This picture of the peasant cross now hangs in our living room challenging us to emulate the fine religious strivings of the Rumanian people who express in simple symbols their search for what is eternal and essential. It represents the Balkan pattern of life at its best, quite as adequately as the pompous Stavropoleos Church in Bucharest, with its Arabo-Byzantine arches; or the sixteenth-century cathedral

of Curtea de Arges, whose triple-barred crosses, gilded
cupolas, twisted towers and Moorish details suggest that its
builders fabricated it from an Oriental fairy tale, which
would have been an acceptable interpretation to Queen
Marie whose burial place it became.

Rumania with its medieval monasteries and robust, decorated churches, finds in the legendary beginning of its capital
a symbol of ancient religious interest. The shepherd Bucur,
leading his flocks to drink by the Dambovita, erected for his
own meditation on that peaceful spot a little hut—as tradition says that Joseph of Arimathea did with his hut of wattles
from which Glastonbury Abbey is said to have ultimately
developed. So, from the rustic shrine of Bucur the shepherd
Bucharest grew with its rugged Balkan crosses.

In Varna, a simple Bulgarian resort town along the Black
Sea, we were prowling about in a dingy shop near the cathedral. The fine specimens of old Macedonian coins attracted Lane's interest but I was lured by the crosses, most
of them heavy silver, crude objects. Among them was a
delicate Greek cross which we purchased. We were leaving
the shop when the burly Bulgarian shopkeeper called us back
to see another small cross. Its primitive silver encased a much
older wooden cross, seen clearly when we turned it over and
noticed its crudely carved Byzantine Christ, with head erect
and feet not crossed. Through the small round arches on the
front of the silver cross, we saw a robed figure well carved
on the obverse of the wooden cross—an unrecognized Father
of the Eastern Church. With what regret must the thrifty
peasant owner of this crude but dignified little emblem have
parted from it as she fondled it on its unusual chain of

square silver mesh! We hope that the satisfaction it affords us partially compensates for the sorrow of its one-time owner.

Far to the north lie countries which border on the *Baltic Sea,* each characterized by a sturdiness which comes from the invigoration of a cold climate. The former republic of Lithuania, now under Russian domination, has for centuries been noted for its choice handcrafts and its amber "Baltic gold." We were happy to add to our collection a simple amber cross whose terminals and etched design are an interesting departure from the plain Latin cross. Although Lithuania is a Roman Catholic country her art is related to Russia, with the addition of her own Baltic peasant patterns.

An exquisitely fashioned replica of a Lithuanian wayside shrine commands admiration. The country's woodcarvers have long been famous. Our symbol was probably perfected on long northern winter evenings. Fashioned of fine-grained yellow wood, its shapely upright is topped by a six-sided, umbrellalike hood crowned by a definitely Byzantine, broad-armed cross widening markedly at its base. In contrast to the massive effect of the cross is the delicacy of skillfully carved northern flowers which spring out from beneath the canopy. No figure of the Redeemer is portrayed. The effect of the whole Lithuanian cross is one of restraint and beauty.

The brilliant silver replica of Danish Queen Dagmar's cross is one of the historic pieces in our collection. Its original is in the Danish Museum of Northern Antiquities. It came into our possession through an American high school youth who flew to Copenhagen to visit his grandfather, carrying with him a sketch we had made of this famous symbol and sufficient money to purchase a Queen Dagmar's cross if he could find one. During his first days in Denmark he searched unsuccessfully, but on the eve of his flight back to New York he located one in a jeweler's shop. With a triumphant grin, he laid the valuable accession on our porch table.

Queen Dagmar's cross is a favorite because it memoralizes a great, good woman originally called Dragomir, "dear peacemaker." She was a daughter of a king of Bohemia and married Waldemar II of Denmark in 1205. The gifts she requested on the morning after her wedding were: liberation of Bishop Waldemar; abolition of the onerous "plow pennies" of the farmers; and freeing of all prisoners. Her interest in social welfare made her the idol of her people. Her name was adapted to Dagmar, Maiden of the Dawn. She died following a Caesarean operation.

Queen Dagmar's cross is a Byzantine type, almost square. On the reverse side it has rounded ends, in each of which is carved a medallion portraying the following figures surrounding a nimbed Byzantine head of Christ: Mary at Christ's right; John at his left; Basil, Bishop of Caesarea (c. A.D. 330–379) above; and the famous Greek Father John Chrysostom (A.D. 354–407) below. These two saints indicate the Byzantine origin of the design. The obverse shows the usual Byzantine Christ with feet not crossed, and it has above his head the letters "IC–XC" ("Jesus Christ").

The original Dagmar's cross is a reliquary pectoral, found on her breast when her tomb was opened around 1690. A facsimile was presented by Frederick II to Princess Alexandra, daughter of King Christian IX of Denmark, who became Queen Alexandra of England.

As the Crusaders swept across Europe they left traces of their thinking and their symbolism in the countries through which they passed. Today the far north country of Finland is still making replicas of Crusaders' crosses. Of the two in our collection one is square and carries a depiction of Jesus wearing a long-sleeved, northern jacket and a crownlike cap topped with a square cross. His arms are extended wide. Its original came to light in northern Finland in an old burial vault dating from the period soon after the Crusades. The other Finnish cross is a modified Latin shape with rounded ends; the feet of Jesus are not crossed as they are in symbols made later. From the base of this cross there hangs a heart on which the timelessness of Christ is signified by an Alpha and Omega on either side of the tall cross. This symbol expresses what has been described as an invincible, hardy courage that heeds no physical barrier—called by the Finns themselves, *sisi*.

The influence of the Crusades is reflected in a number of the northern crosses whose forms are being widely reproduced today. Christianity entered Scandinavia even before it penetrated Germany and the Rhineland regions which owed conversion to Boniface of England. By A.D. 1000 Christianity was sweeping into Scandinavia. King Olaf persuaded the crew of Leif Ericson to be baptized, and imposed upon Leif the responsibility of carrying Christianity into Greenland. Our Norwegian cross is the square type, whose ends are gracefully rounded. Each arm is adorned with a fan of conventionalized palm leaf, for victory.

The handsome doors that enclose the Security Council Room at the United Nations headquarters in New York are meaningful. Although the cross as symbol is not apparent anywhere in this meeting place of political and spiritual cross currents, the carved doors of the room furnished by Norway are significant to those who observe them. They carry, inlaid in silver and wood, the symbol of crosslike daggers with what look like anchors of hope turning themselves around the daggers. The motifs of the draperies which line the Security Council Room, also a gift of Norway, alternate the sheaf of wheat, denoting to Christians God's bounty, and the concealed anchor cross of early Roman catacombs iconography, but adding details which may possibly signify Norwegian mountains, hearts, or harpoons. After all, symbols are what the observer sees in them as well as what the maker intends them to be.

Iceland, volcanic island situated close to the Arctic Circle in the North Atlantic, carries upon its flag a red unequal-armed cross superimposed upon a white cross and laid sideways upon a blue field—a symbol derived from Denmark. This predominantly Evangelical Lutheran country, which has no army, navy, or forts—and no illiteracy—was an independent republic as early as 930. Iceland's Parliament (*Athling*) observed its one thousandth anniversary in 1930.

Another rugged cross is a Carpatho-Polish one, showing a marked Byzantine influence, as we might expect from the remote Hukul people deriving from the region of the Caspian Sea.

Legacies from other European Countries

ITALIAN CROSSES of the Renaissance have small intrinsic value compared with the Byzantine and Crusaders crosses. Nevertheless, they have given us much inspiration because they are linked with Italian cities which disseminated religious art in the two centuries between Dante's vision in 1300 and the fall of Florence in 1530.

We turn with enthusiasm to certain characteristics of the Renaissance, at which time artists broke away from the rigidity of mosaic and depicted their love of life and their religion of joy in frescoes of Giotto in Padua, and in paintings of Fra Angelico on the walls of San Marco Monastery, Florence. This latter artist emphasized the hospitality of his Dominican order by painting a lunette over a cloister doorway—a nimbed Christ with long, fair hair, being welcomed into the Monastery by two friars. The same charm of form which Fra Angelico painted in his Monastery fresco of "The Annunciation," his "Madonna and Child," and his golden

angels, he gave to his "Crucifixion," where he brought into
the new beauty of the Renaissance an old symbol for the
atonement, a white pelican above Christ's head. It would
have been impossible for Fra Angelico to make even a Golgotha devoid of beauty. He was a true son of the Renaissance.

Several of our *Italian* crosses have color as their chief
charm—that glowing, pleasant color we always associate
with travels up and down the peninsula between the Adriatic and the Tyrrhenian. One cross, carved from a single
piece of coral, is beveled with eleven little faceted squares,
one for each of the faithful disciples, and all crowned by a
tiny pilgrim shell. The colors remind us of the warm red
walls of Pompeian villas in the shadow of Vesuvius; or of the
harvest of oval tomatoes waiting under their shelter of trail-
ing grapes.

The deep blue cross from Santa Margherita on the Gulf
of Genoa looks more like a flower with four slender sapphire-
colored petals covered with a filigree of silver frost, than
a cross. Each time we hold this glass treasure up to the
light, we feel as if we were looking through a medieval cathedral window. It is a suitable neighbor to the gracefully
tapering mosaic cross we found near Genoa's Crusader Cathedral of San Lorenzo with its own Crusaders crosses
worked into marble façade. This Genoese cross looks as if
stones of chalcedony had been hammered into the almost
invisible tesserae which make the background for finely
wrought white mosaic flowers, the whole comprising a design as pure and simple as the blue and white Della Robbia
medallions of the Bambino in Florence. At the center of this
colorful cross there is a circle filled with what look like dust-

sized particles of ground ruby, background for a white dove, symbolic of the Holy Spirit.

Our Bologna cross, one of the cheapest so far as price is concerned, is charming in color and shape. Of black and white enamel in alternating stripes, its arms of equal length terminating in shapely fleurs-de-lis making it a cross patonce, this will always speak of the Renaissance university center of Bologna where we found it. Dante and Giotto were graduates of this oldest university in Europe, whose ten thousand students gave its community a proud title, "The Learned City." But in addition to her university and her strange twelfth-century towers, Bologna has a number of interesting churches, including the Church of San Domenico, where the founder of the Dominican order is buried.

As we approached this thirteenth-century church we noticed an unusual square cross over its portal. Later we secured a replica from the brother who showed us the great carved altarpiece with a fourteenth-century crucifix lifted by its highest pinnacle; and the famous Arca di San Domenico, the shrine executed by Niccola Pisano and Fra Guglielmo to contain the sarcophagus of Dominic.

As I look at the contrasting black and white enamel pattern of our Bologna cross I recall that the Black Friars of the Dominican Order wear white garments beneath their black capes—perhaps part of the symbolism of the Bologna cross.

In this same period William I (the Bad) of Sicily was bringing Moslem mosaicists from the East to adorn his palace and its Capella Reale, the most ornate chapel in the world located at Palermo; and William II (the Good) was lifting into the sun-swept air of Monreale a cathedral whose mosaics depict the sweep of Biblical history from Old Testament times through the Resurrection of Jesus. Seventy thousand square feet of mosaic Bible stories incorporate the chief symbols of Christian belief. The giant head and shoulders of the Byzantine, regal, wide-awake Christ completely fill the half dome of the tribune of the cathedral which is built in the form of a Latin cross. There is in our collection a cheerful mosaic cross bought at the Cathedral of Monreale, Sicily.

The mosaics of Monreale are almost twice as extensive as those of Venice, yet these Sicilian jewels cannot exceed the glory of the façade of the Basilica of San Marco. The forgotten artists, through their cubes of colored glass or stone overlaid with glass and untarnishing gold leaf, tell the triumph of Christ as he carries his victorious cross in the lunette above the center door. This tall, resplendent cross is carried in the left arm of the Saviour, as if it were his scepter. He sits enthroned between his mother and Mark, with right hand uplifted to scatter blessings of God upon admiring throngs of people awed by the gold and azure glories of the sacred mosaics.

The Basilica of San Marco was begun in the early Middle Ages to enshrine the body of John Mark. Modeled after the Church of the Holy Apostles at Constantinople and completed in 1094, it was considered an architectural masterpiece. It was regarded not only as a mausoleum but as a monument to the maritime power of Venice, whose merchants and Crusaders brought from the East all the columns, Byzantine marbles, and bas-reliefs their cargo ships could carry—many of these being given in return for aid to the Byzantine emperor in his war against Moslems in Sicily. From the ninth century through the eleventh, wealth was lavished on San Marco, which glorifies the symbol of the cross as few other churches in Christendom today. Its Greek architects designed the Basilica in the form of an almost square Byzantine cross, whose center and arms are topped by superb Byzantine domes which, seen from the balcony of the Clock Tower, look as if made of crinkled bronze-green paper. Nowhere can one find a church where more crosses are worked into its fabric. In dark nooks on capitals of columns brought from vanished churches of Asia Minor, carved on walls, incised in marble work on façade and in the nave, in undulating mosaics where people kneel in prayer on the damp floor—everywhere are crosses of Christ. There is also plenty of Byzantine symbolism, as the bas-relief of twelve sheep flanked by palms of victory, like the bas-relief we saw in Istanbul, excavated from an earlier Hagia Sophia. There are peacocks of immortality carved in the marble parapet of an upper gallery; griffins, symbolic of persecutors; the cunning fox; the temperate donkey; the eagle, symbolic of the Resurrection—all tucked into the dark corners of San Marco. But all of this fine imagery leads to the cross, conspicuous on the great rood in front of the altar.

This impressive gilt Latin-type crucifix carries in its trefoil ends the symbolic lion of St. Mark and an eagle denoting the Resurrection of Jesus. It is unique in having fifteen wide-open fleurs-de-lis springing from the terminations of the cross, each fleur-de-lis concealing in its leaves three cones, symbolic of eternal life.

In the Treasury of San Marco we were impressed by several Byzantine silver reliquaries and book covers telling in enamel and stones the story of the Crucifixion. One of these, a Lorraine cross, surrounded by jewels, was brought West

after the Fourth Crusade. Another, carried back by Henry
of Flanders, encases in precious metal what he supposed to
be a part of the wood of the "true cross" obtained in Constantinople. Another cross of venerable wood, encased in a
later cross, bears messages in Greek affixed to its arms. It is
identified as a cross of the Empress Irene, brought to Venice
by Crusaders from Constantinople in 1204.

We are fortunate to have in our collection a small, hand-
somely carved silver miniature of the Byzantine bronze chan-
delier which hangs at the center of San Marco's nave. Lane
found it one day in a shop near the Basilica and we treasure it
as a reminder of that tremendous Eastern cross, intersected
by another of similar design, which lights the way of worshipers walking in the medieval darkness of this church.

In San Marco one sees the greatness of Venetian art before
the Renaissance gave the world its Bellini, Titian, Tintoretto,
whose masterpieces testify to the new breath of life and enthusiasm for religion embodying Renaissance freedom of
spirit, unloosed from medieval swaddling bands. The crude
cryptograms of the catacombs were gone; medieval symbol-
isms also. Madonnas now were real mothers; the Child aglow
with beauty and charm. The "Ecce Homo" of Guido Reni was
a thorn-crowned Man, as well as a redeeming Lord.

The intersecting square crosses which top the five
"crinkled" domes that rise from the roof of San Marco always
astonish beholders who see them from the Piazza below, or
from the adjacent Clock Tower with its Gog and Magog who
hammer out the golden hours. These crosses against the sky
are unique. Each arm terminates in a group of three balls,
which could be considered symbolic of the moneyed in-
terests of Venetian merchants who flung their enterprises

across the wide expanse of the Mediterranean during and after the Crusades.

But there is another meaning possible, based on the legend of St. Nicholas, the fourth-century Bishop of Myra in Asia Minor who lives in mosaics within the Basilica, wearing a stole adorned with Eastern crosses. Nicholas, friend of the poor, delighted to give presents to children; to save sailors from perils of the sea; and to encourage such people as the poor man of his native town whose three daughters were betrothed but could not marry because they had no dowries. The story runs that Nicholas, passing the poor man's home one night, tossed in three ball-like round bags of gold—one for each daughter. This same St. Nicholas is the patron saint of Dutch sailors and has an anchor for his symbol; he is also the saint who became the Christmas St. Nicholas. His legend is honored in a stained-glass window in the Chartres Cathedral. The lancet depicts the haloed Nicholas, the grateful father, and the daughters overwhelmed as they behold the disklike round sacks each bearing a Jerusalem cross.

Most collectors of crosses turn to Florence for accessions, especially to the Ponte Vecchio with its silversmiths' shops which have sold crosses for centuries. These we appreciate— especially if studded with ovals of lapis lazuli from Russian mines. But from a pushcart near the Uffizi Gallery we got a prized replica of a Byzantine "inhabited" cross—carved with people participating in Passion Week. Six square panels depict the scenes of Christ's last days.

The carnelian-studded cross in our collection which was bought in Rome holds special significance because it was purchased the day Lane had an audience with Pope Pius XII, an audience which he desired in order that he, a Christian

minister, might observe this spiritual leader of a large segment of Christianity.

Many of the world's most valued crosses are housed in the
Treasury of St. Peter's and in the Vatican Museum. We have
especially appreciated the Byzantine cross of the Eastern
emperor, Justinus II, made probably in the sixth century;
and Michelangelo's famous statue of Jesus carrying his cross
in the church of Santa Maria Sopre. The gigantic Cross of
the Martyrs in the Colosseum is overwhelming in its sacred
historic significance. It hallows the scene where Christian
martyrs were sacrificed to beasts during gladiatorial contests
in this largest Roman amphitheater—completed after the fire
of A.D. 217 on the site of part of Nero's Golden House. The
cross, however, dates from our own century.

Excavations below the Vatican crypts have revealed tombs
having popular pagan symbols for life—peacocks, acanthus
leaves, cherubim, Bacchantes, cornucopias of poppy stalk,
birds, eschatological monsters. But they have also given us one
of the early depictions of the cross in Rome, rating from
c. A.D. 340, on the lid of a sarcophagus excavated in the Grotto
Nuove. The cross forms part of a scene, "The Adoration of
the Magi," with resplendent camels and angels. Behind the
Virgin is a tall cross presented frontally, and without a base—
a unique motif in Christian sepulchral art, telling in a nativity
work of Christ's ultimate triumph through the cross.

But, as recounted in *The Biblical Archaeologist*, Vol. XII,
1949, perhaps the oldest iconic evidence thus far found in
the early Vatican crypts is a small mausoleum, in the middle
of whose vault is a *Christus Helios*, superseding Apollo the
sun god. This *Christus*, carried forward in his chariot by four

horses, is Apollolike but actually represents *Christus sol iustitiae*—Christ the sun of justice, or of salvation.

In the catacombs of Rome, the cross is not rare, nor is it found in great numbers—some twenty or so is the estimate of one authority who claims that square Greek crosses dating from the second century have been found, and an unequal-armed cross from the third century. Older than the cross as we usually visualize it is the anchor, which can easily express a concealed cross. In fact, the cross is one of the later Christian funerary forms to develop. The anchor and the fish (ichthus) were both employed earlier. Sometimes the Crucifixion was depicted without use of any cross, but showing Christ as an *orans* between two thieves, as in the Monza Ampoules.

Moving over the waters of the blue Mediterranean we come to *France* the art-loving, France the skillful-fingered, France the creator of intricate beauty—whether it be a Chartres Cathedral, or a Chenonceaux Chateau; a Bourgereau "Nativity" or a Rodin's "Hand of God." France is appropriately represented in our collection by some of our most handsome crosses.

One we call "The General's Heirloom." It has a World War I history, this ancient, frail, deep yellow, solid gold cross, dainty with the art which only a French goldsmith can achieve. Before the United States entered World War I, an American woman physician from Pittsburgh enlisted to drive a French ambulance to the Front. One Christmas Eve, after she had been hauling wounded boys to dressing stations, she suddenly felt Christ's presence more real than ever before. Although she was the daughter of Methodist missionaries,

she had never had any definite religious experience. But that
Christmas Eve at the Front, the White Comrade spoke to her
and claimed her as one who was doing his work. Finding
herself surrounded by pious French Catholics when the
great experience came, she walked to a barn which had been
converted into a chapel and there declared her desire to become a member of the Roman Catholic Church.

A famous French general became her godfather. Shortly
after, he presented her with an antique gold cross of choice
workmanship which he had sent an ófficer to bring from his
chateau near Rheims. When the doctor returned to America
to say farewell to her friends before plunging permanently
into medical work in the slums of Paris as a sister of St. Vincent de Paul, she came to our home. As she was leaving she
thrust the general's golden cross into my mother's hands.

"I am not permitted to carry this treasure with me," she
said. "A simple ebony cross will be my only one. Keep this.
It is my dearest earthly possession."

The general's heirloom is rolled so thin, and worn still
thinner by prayerful use, that we hesitate to lift it lest it
crack, as indeed the trefoil at its base has already done. It is a
Latin crucifix bearing the figure of Christ. And, with French
art which tries to soften the agony by beautifying it, the
board above his head, carved with the "INRI" ("Jesus of
Nazareth, King of the Jews"), has been surrounded with
flowers. The ends of this French cross are floriated with designs unlike any other we have seen. They look like scrolls
worked into concealed fleurs-de-lis, for purity. Yet they also
resemble gold harps.

On the reverse side, several sets of initials have been engraved, erased, and re-engraved, denoting successive owners.

How we wonder who "M.B." was and under what circumstances she or he received this cross! Those two initials by their careful workmanship stand out as a part of the original goldsmith's design. Others are more crudely scratched.

A companion to the American woman doctor's French cross is a small silver one presented to us years later by an elderly lady who had served as nurse during one of the fiery battles of the Marne, and received from her commanding officer this cross of courage.

One Christmas there came into our collection a handsome gold cross which had been sold in New York as Russian. Its elegance of design almost conceals the fact that it is a cross. But under its decoration of brilliant white stones, and behind its intersecting spear points which have been worked into fleurs-de-lis, we saw that it is really two crosses, a square one at the top, which becomes the upper half of a Latin cross, terminating in a heart-shaped brilliant. The wide loop by which it hangs from its chain dates it as being at least a century or two old. It has become so thin that wearing it is a risk.

We found an unexpected clue to its identity months later as we were peering into the windows of Gibraltar's main street, that most curious narrow passageway where wares from everywhere turn up. In a small shop window was a gold cross, the shape of our "Russian" one, but of more recent workmanship. It was adorned with beautifully cut green stones.

"Well!" we exclaimed to the antiquarian. "You have a Russian cross like ours!"

"No, lady," replied the Gibraltan. "This is a Spanish cross from Cordova. A refugee fleeing over the border begged me to buy it. She was starving. Would I not take it for a few shillings? Yes, it is indeed a Spanish cross and a very fine one. It is the most aristocratic one in my shop."

But its real identity came one day after our return home from that summer of Mediterranean meanderings. By chance we opened the *Encyclopaedia Britannica* to the section, "Jewelry." There we found a picture of this cross, labeled "a French-Norman pendant cross."

Our group of French crosses was augmented one day by a Huguenot cross, presented by a member of the Huguenot Society. It is basically Byzantine, but added to it as a pendant is the emblem of the dove, signifying the Holy Spirit.

None of our French crosses has provoked more interest than a small modified Maltese ivory cross from Paris. At its center it has a magnifying glass one-eighth of an inch in diameter, such as the French delight to fashion. Holding this close to the eye, the beholder sees a young Christ, carrying the world on his heart; and on the world, a tall cross. The eye follows the inscription, *"Saveur du monde."* The cross of Christ is magnified when people make an effort to behold it; but the cross in turn magnifies those who find it.

On his last journey to the Mediterranean, Lane found in Nice a typical French Provençal cross in faïence signed by the artist. Its arms are broad and substantial and from the center of its shining black surface rises a gold heart.

Two square, silver-edged *German* iron crosses from World War I and World War II have come into our collection. The Iron Cross distributed during World War I carries on its face an imperial crown at the top, the date 1914 at the bottom and "W" for Wilhelm at its center; on its reverse, a crown, initials "F W" for Friederich Wilhelm; a cluster of oak leaves with acorn at center, and at bottom, 1813.

Iron Crosses distributed during World War II were, appropriately, larger than those awarded in World War I. They carry a hooked cross, swastika, on the face; and on the reverse, "1813," obviously the date of founding of the Order of the Iron Cross.

Our specimen of Adolph Hitler's War Mothers' Cross is, from an aesthetic viewpoint, one of the most beautiful in the collection. Fashioned in graceful shape of deep blue and white enamel and silver, its intersection is shot through with a bundle of silver light rays. But at its heart there is the swastika of Hitlerism, surrounded by a circle carrying the inscription, *Der Deutschen Mütter* ("To the German Mothers"). The inscription on the reverse reads, "16 Dezember 1938," and the autograph "A. Hitler." War Mothers' crosses of gold with enamel were distributed to mothers of very large families; crosses of baser metals to mothers of smaller families.

The Elizabeth cross, secured in the Elizabethankirche of purest Early Gothic style, erected 1236–83 by the Grand Master of the Teutonic Order, honors the memory of a German noblewoman of such charitable activities that she died of overexertion. She is buried in the Elizabethankirche and is remembered as "St. Elizabeth of Hungary, wife of the landgrave Louis." Although her silver-gilt sarcophagus is still seen in the church, her body was long ago moved to an undiscovered portion of the structure by the Protestant enthusiasm of Philip the Generous. Elizabeth and her cross deserve to be thought of together with noble Queen Dagmar of Denmark, whose elegant cross has been already described.

Most reverent of our German crosses is an exquisite one paved with deep red garnets. Secured two generations ago by an American, the father of a now aged friend of ours, and given to her when she was a little girl, this lovely emblem of the living Christ speaks not only the pious Christian faith of the "Old Germany," but also denotes the radiant new spiritual devotion alive in modern Germany among families loyal to Christ.

Our collection of crosses includes a few emblems of nations which suffered at the hands of Hitlerism. There is an *Austrian* cross brought from Oberammergau by one who had attended a performance of the Passion Play. This slender, gleaming silver cross carries at its heart the dates "1634–1934," marking the tercentenary performance of the historic drama of Christ's eternal sacrifice for man. The ends of its beams are barbed and its intersection is bounded by a broken circle whose upper portion becomes the top of the long winding sheet used during the Play to lower Christ's body from the cross. Six light rays of glory crown the top of the circling sheet.

Poland is represented among our crosses by a small bronze cross pattée of modified proportions approaching Byzantine lines. It carries a Latin cross superimposed at its center, and it is crowned by another small Latin cross.

Czechoslovakia is represented by a broad-armed Latin cross, decorated with small roses. It comes from the Moravian region, homeland of devout Christians who profoundly influenced John Wesley.

At Gibraltar we found an old *Spanish* silver cross with two parallel arms, a patriarchal type, with four bundles of intersecting rays of hope emerging from two crowns of thorns; its terminations, those of a cross fleury, have wide-open petals symbolizing the mature Christian. It came from Burgos, headquarters of General Franco's government during the Spanish Civil War.

Two years later, after the close of the war, in the little port city of Vigo on the Atlantic coast we found a cheap metal cross. It was one of many being sold to people still drinking the dregs of war, people who had stood in line for hours waiting for the bitter brown bread or who had clamored in the market place for a few small fish—while their town was set in the midst of grain fields and on the edge of an ocean yielding an unlimited supply of fish. That evening the people thronged into the cathedral for this was the feast day of the Christ of Victory, and the finely wrought altar crucifix would be carried through the streets with thousands following it. Was not peace the work of the Vigo Christ of Victory? The few last pesetas that might have bought bread were spent instead for a tall candle to carry in the procession and the people went away content. Their sons had been killed at Valencia but victory had been won. Food could be had some other time—perhaps.

Our Caravaca Spanish cross was made in that little town in southeastern Spain known for its medieval Castle of the Holy Cross and for its church housing a famous crucifix, which is carried through the streets every May in recognition of its healing power. It is a brass reliquary of the type affixed to doorways of old Caravaca houses, whose occupants say, "When the two parts of the reliquary open of their own accord, a storm is brewing." It has two wide transverse bars, as the patriarchal and the Lorraine crosses have, suggesting, according to one interpretation, Christ's ministry to Jews and Gentiles; and two short transverse bars, one making a little pedestal, the other a bar across the upright to receive the loop. On one side is carved a figure of Mary standing lightly on the crescent moon, as in the famous painting by Murillo, "The Immaculate Conception." The moon denotes the worshipful attitude of all nature, supplemented by the adoration of angels surrounding Mary. Our interpretation of this side of our cross is the eternal identification of the mother with the sufferings of her son, in Jesus' time and in every age.

On the reverse side of the Caravaca cross is an elaborate depiction of all the elements of the Golgotha tragedy. Beneath a crown of thorns on the topmost bar, the head and arms of Christ, accompanied by two angels, rest on the center transverse, with his feet affixed by a single nail to the third bar intersecting the upright about halfway to its top. This leaves room on the lower section of the upright for the traditional three nails, with a halo about them and a cherub above; and a strident rooster, reminiscent of Peter's warning cock. At the foot of the cross are two iron-studded flagellation scourges. Right and left of the feet of Christ are a ladder by which he was elevated, hammer and pliers, spear, a sponge on a reed, and Judas' lantern. Certainly a sufficiently graphic dramatization to please even a Byzantine symbolist.

From Cordova, Spain, by way of a pawnshop in Malaga, we secured a silver cross, whose filigree is so lacelike and so worn with age that it is falling apart. Its conventional design of delicate openwork and its round beaded dots suggest the skilled Moorish craftsmen with their Moslem abhorrence of idolatry, who were summoned from Damascus to work on the Cordova mosque, now the Cathedral. These tenth-century architects erected the twelve hundred arched pillars in twenty-nine aisles, ornamented them with ten tons of mosaic tesserae from Constantinople, lighted the mosque with almost five thousand graceful glass lamps, and tucked into every available surface the geometric designs of Islamic art. Ever since that far-off century, Cordova has been noted for its silversmiths, an influence going back to Syrian and Byzantine sources.

In the rugged mountains of Andalusia, between Gibraltar and Malaga, is the strange Spanish town of Ronda, whose Palace of the Moorish Kings stands on the rim of an extinct volcano. It is such a site as Moors would choose for a fastness, for in its narrow gorge, the *tajo* of the Guadiaro River, five hundred feet deep and three hundred feet wide, citizens protected themselves from enemies approaching by the fertile plain. Ronda has always been the stronghold of men of extreme political convictions, but it also has its pleasant craft shops. In one of these we found a Ronda bronze cross.

In Malaga, near the old Promenade, we found a little brass cross which appeals because its stubby upper arm is intersected by well-fashioned bundles of rays, indicating the intention of its designer to present a resurrection cross. On many a church altar, in America and elsewhere, this is a favorite cross, for its sunburst speaks the Easter hope, revealed when three Marys "very early on the first day of the week . . . when the sun had risen," came to the Garden and found the empty tomb of the risen Lord.

From Barcelona, largest Mediterranean port, came our last Spanish cross—a little black and gold one carrying Moorish conventional designs and having at its center the sacred initials "JHS" with a small Latin cross rising from the "H."

From Spain we came into prosperous, neutral *Portugal,* a great country of which many foreigners know little. It has been an independent state since the twelfth century. Its dominant religion is Roman Catholic but it grants freedom of worship.

The strategic location of its capital, Lisbon, with a fine port on the Tagus River used by ships and air-borne craft, makes for commercial prosperity. Its streets are clean, its parks beautifully kept, its people well dressed. Its shops are filled with well-made modern wares. Neat, buxom Portuguese fish-wives stride contentedly through market sections, carrying on their heads flat baskets of long, silver fish. Brazilian coffee fills the air.

But dominating the scene is the unique Church of the Hieronymites (Jeronimos), with its long ivory-colored façade in the Manueline style, and its exuberant Late Gothic arched cloisters unlike any others in Europe. Just as we were going into this famous church the silver wings of an airplane carrying mail for New York whirred overhead and disappeared into the clouds. It flashed above the site from which Vasco da Gama sailed in his slow ship of epochal discovery which established a route around South Africa to spice-laden India, opening up trade routes which enriched not only Portugal, but all of Europe. The explorer's prayer, lifted in the Belem (Bethlehem) section of Lisbon on the night before sailing, was answered. He returned home safely in 1429. The site of the chapel he used—erected by Prince Henry the Navigator—is incorporated in the precincts of the magnificent church which contains the remains of Da Gama, who kept compass and cross close together.

On top of the church, the national Portuguese cross stands traced against the sky, topping the emblem of Portuguese explorers, a globe with a girdle across it. This cross is some-what pattée, its flattened ends broadening out from a cross of

Latin proportions. A plain Latin cross is superimposed upon it. Fashioned in red and white, the national colors, and outlined in gold, the cross of Portugal is impressive.

The last cross Lane selected was a stately Portuguese filigree fleury one, whose color suggested the rich tone of a marine sunset. He had it in his pocket when he went up forward on his ship as it put out from Lisbon for New York.

An old Portuguese sailor joined him and remarked, "We are out in the Atlantic now. Gibraltar and the Mediterranean are far behind."

"Yes," Lane agreed, "I wonder what is ahead of us now?"

Island Crosses. The insularity of island peoples has developed individuality in symbolism. Several islands have contributed types of the cross to iconographic materials. The crosses of *Iona* are described with Scottish crosses.

The mid-Mediterranean fortress island of rock-bastioned *Malta* has given its name to one of the most distinctive and best-known forms of cross—the Maltese. This symbol is of the square variety, having fishtail, indented ends. Its arms taper toward the intersection. The eight points gave rise to the term "Knights of the Eight-Pointed Cross"—brave warriors of the military order of St. John, called "The Knights Hospitaler" because of their founding hospitals for sick pilgrims to Palestine and elsewhere on the pilgrim route from Europe to the Near East.

The Maltese cross is emblazoned throughout the Church of St. John at Valetta, where heraldic symbols enrich tombs of the Grand Masters. But probably these are less significant to Christian travelers than is St. Paul's Bay, seven miles northwest of Valetta, where occurred the shipwreck of the Apostle who, after sailing for Rome, and being threatened with catastrophe, "noticed a bay with a beach" (Acts 27:39) but struck "a shoal."

To the Knights of St. John, Charles V granted the island of Malta, 58 miles south of Sicily and about 187 miles from the North African coast. The Knights, driven from Syria in 1310, established headquarters in Rhodes, from which they were expelled by Moslem Turks in 1522 after having exerted a lasting influence through their Christian ministry and architectural genius, which is seen today embodied in stalwart towers, walls, moats, palaces, public structures, including the Hospital of the Knights with its dramatic grand staircase.

Rhodes, reconstructed by expert Italian artist-engineers with an instinctive sense of history, is adorned with Rhodian crosses of St. John. On the Street of the Knights the doors of the Grand Masters and knights of England and Spain and France are emblazoned with coats-of-arms embodying their favorite square cross. Inside the great Hospice of the Knights for sick pilgrims, the martial monks lavished the cross, especially in the lower cloister whose round Crusader arches spring from square pillars to support a stone-vaulted ceiling, and in the spacious upper portico reached by a flight of broad steps. The sick who were carried up here first tested their returning strength in that upper gallery outside their cells. What rejoicing when they were able to join the other patients in the Large Refectory—very long for its slender width, its windows high up near a roof supported by seven round pillars, on each of whose capitals is carved a square cross.

The Rhodian cross is square, Maltese in type, and having at its center a little antelope around which is a crown of foliage, with the usual intersecting spear points transformed into four twigs of leaves "for the healing of the nations."

The Rhodian cross takes us into the heart of the heraldry popularized by the Knights Hospitaler of St. John of Jerusalem and the Knights Templar who went to free Holy Places from entrenched Moslems.

Heraldry in Europe received its main impact from the Crusaders who, accustomed to advancing into battle against the Moslems with pennons flying, returned home and established some of the great houses extant today and gave them their cross-emblazoned coats-of-arms. The first English king to have arms on his shield was Richard I, in 1189. From the thirteenth century on, the popularity of shields increased and many of them were adorned with crosses, the most beautiful being the square cross-crosslet, of which there are ten on the coat-of-arms of the Earl of Warwick. When knights in France and England rode out to the jousting tournaments, their cross-trimmed arms were gorgeous to behold. They grew accustomed to the cross on their armor, their swords, and about their necks on heavy chains, stitched upon their flags and saddle cloths, and on their lances in cavalry attacks. Often the ground plans for their churches in Palestine were in the form of a cross, as at Emmaus. Indeed, they became so cross-minded that, like the civilians who thronged the Pilgrim Roads between Europe and Palestine, they felt unprotected without a cross from the Land of the Cross, forgetting that Christ is a Spirit and needs no such symbol to assure his being "in the midst" of those who desire his presence to guide.

Another island cross we found in beautiful Funchal, capital

of the *Madeira* islands, an integral part of Portugal. This delicate little square cross is a perfect Maltese, with the eight-pointed indented ends tapering toward the center, symbolic of the eight Beatitudes. At its heart in fine blue enamel is a flower, typical of this island paradise floating in Atlantic mists. This cross is a perfect example of the way in which local areas work their characteristics into their symbols, for at dawn on those days when shiploads of travelers are to weigh anchor at this island, flower women worship in the small Funchal cathedral whose gable is topped with its flower-centered Madeira cross.

Another island cross comes from the West Indies island of *Martinique*, home of Napoleon's Empress Josephine. In 1902 its chief commercial city Saint-Pierre suffered a volcanic eruption which buried it under burning lava and ash. Much of the area has never been wholly rescued from the rubble. One day an American businessman, walking among the old debris stirring up rubble with his cane, saw a metal object protruding above the mass. Drawing it out, he found it to be a crucifix. Knowing of our interest in historic crosses, he placed his Martinique, volcano-buried emblem in our collection.

Our last island cross came from *Corfu*, where Lane found it on a rugged ride through this Greek island in the Ionian Sea. The symbol shares the barbaric beauty of the mountainous olive-clad terrain. It is worked in heavy silver studded with four red and one green stone worn smooth with pious use. Two spears intersect where the arms meet. Small wheel-like pendants dangle from transverse and upright.

Crosses of the British Isles

DURING one of those diagonal English rains which look best when seen aslant a cathedral spire, we stood in the cloister of Salisbury and contemplated spires lifting four hundred feet of gray grace against a grayer sky.

We commented on the fact that although British cathedrals have a wide variety of gable crosses they do not have spires topped by crosses of cathedral proportions. When we mentioned the fact to a citizen of Salisbury who, like us, had taken the rainy morning to enjoy the cathedral, he countered by telling us how entrancing the cloister is by moonlight and hoped we had not missed the lush marvel of the Cathedral Green that watery morning. Then he added, "But even if our cathedrals are not crowned by crosses, you will find many a rood worked into their gables or their fabric, as are the nineteen consecration crosses on buttresses and walls of this cathedral. And it is always impressive to see a simple cross lifted up by its carved rood screen as your eye looks beyond it from the choir, or beholds it down the vast sweep of nave, under a beautiful groined ceiling."

We agreed, for we had seen this very effect here at Salisbury.

He continued, "And as for crosses, it would pay you to see two old Saxon ones at Romsey Abbey, yonder, as you go from Salisbury to Winchester."

Romsey is a pleasant little town to come upon, even in a dreary English rain, for it lies in that gentle Hampshire countryside where cottages with beetling brows of thatch stand inside thickets of flowers shielded from the road by hedges of dripping beauty. Stretches of woods—oak, beech, evergreen, elm, woven together with tall-plumed bracken—filter daylight through leaves and provide a cathedral sanctity which is refreshing for those who drive.

Even in the rain, the small square-built stone abbey impressed us as being as fine a small Norman church as we had seen in England. Its low square central tower, its round-arched windows, date its construction in the twelfth century when Normans were building brilliantly in England. Seldom did they excel the simple beauty of their round arches in the choir and transept of Romsey Abbey or in the vaulting of its south aisle. But we were bent this morning on finding the two Saxon crosses in this old Abbey founded by King Edward the Elder in A.D. 907 for nuns of the Benedictine Order.

We recalled the early Saxon abbesses of Romsey as we stepped from the graceful Abbess Door into the Cloister and saw the Romsey Rood, carved in stone sheltered by a little pointed gable. Affixed to the stone wall of the cloister, this "Living Christ" from Saxon or early Norman times at once revealed itself as belonging to the Byzantine type Christ of the Mediterranean world. As this type of crucifix died out in England early in the eleventh century its presence here is unique. Its survival of the Reformation is perhaps due to the fact that when the Cloister was destroyed a shed was built on the site and for centuries nobody noticed the crucifix on the outer wall. Above the head of Christ the hand of God is descending, denoting the Father. Inside the Abbey in the South Choir Aisle we saw another Saxon cross. It uses the Byzantine manner of dramatizing the Crucifixion by placing right and left of the living Christ a group of witnesses, Mary, John, and two Roman soldiers, one thrusting the spear to pierce the side of Christ, the other lifting the hyssop reed. The Romsey crosses illustrate how "immigrant" art ideas were brought in by prelates who had visited Rome and caught the details of Byzantine symbolism, or had traveled farther to centers of Eastern Christianity.

Coming into Romsey Square we were pleased to find in a musty bookshop a small brass replica of the Saxon rood. This cross reminds us of a tradition about the first abbess with the lovely Saxon name of Aethelfleda who was so spiritual that if a gust of English wind extinguished her candle while she was reading Scripture to her nuns, she went on uninterrupted, supplied with light by the mystical glow that radiated from her fingertips. Typical, this, of romantic Romsey.

Queen Elizabeth II and her husband, the Duke of Edinburgh, worshiped in Romsey's ancient church on the Sunday after their marriage.

Like our cross from Romsey Abbey, one of our Cornish

types is associated with a woman, Buryana. While we were driving from Penzance to Land's End we came into a village whose wayside cross in the churchyard arrested our attention. A pleasing square Cornish cross it is, which looks as if it had once crowned a taller upright. The carved figure upon it is almost effaced by weather. But it recalls a saintly Irish woman who was honored by the Saxon King Athelstan who, departing in 930 for his conquest of the Scilly Isles, vowed that if he returned safely he would here build a church and dedicate it to Buryana. And so he did. Its story has become a well-known part of Land's End where the very rocks have romantic Cornish names—The Irish Lady, The Plumed Knight, and Pulpit Rock where John Wesley preached above the roar of the Atlantic as it beat in upon the English headland.

We were gratified that little St. Buryana's village had made replicas of its Cornish cross, in bluish native stone. One of these was tucked into our luggage as we went on to Sennen, "last town in England."

The market cross was a distinctive feature of thriving medieval English towns. At first erected in yards of monasteries where moneys were received and sermons preached, the crosses were later removed to the intersection of thoroughfares, the community gathering place as well as market center. One of the finest is Winchester's Butter Cross, a carved Gothic canopy mounted on several steps and tipped by a cross. As we looked at its fountain we recalled the quaint story of its predecessor, where merchants, in time of plague, asked customers to leave their money in the basin of flowing water from which coins safeguarded from pollution were collected at night. Salisbury's market cross with buttresses rising from its rounded arcade looked to us like the crown of an Alfred or an Ethelbert. The base of the market cross at little Epworth where John Wesley preached to throngs still stands, but it has lost its symbol.

All of these old market crosses may have been designed to influence fair trade; for this same purpose Dalmatian Dubrovnik carved a Latin inscription over the scales of the sixteenth-century Customs House: "With whatsoever scale ye weigh to others, God will weigh you."

Another cross in our collection has its background in Saxon times—and earlier. It comes from the Hampshire cathedral town of Winchester, occupied by Saxons as early as the fifth century, when Cedric ruled. When Egbert was there crowned King of Britain in the ninth century, it became capital of the realm and so remained for three hundred years. Saxons, who had been nomadic tillers of the land, moved into the vicinity of the walled town they called Wintanceaster, as glad for its protection by night as they were to go forth to till their acres by day. It was a long step from these simple folk to Alfred the Great, first well-known English king, who wrote his noted *Anglo-Saxon Chronicle* at Winchester.

But our Winchester cross has nothing to do with either Saxon kings or even the cathedral founded by them in the tenth century and enlarged by so many successive builders that it reflects every period of English cathedral architecture: Norman, Tudor, and Renaissance. We found our little silver cross potent in a unique institution in Winchester, known as The Hospital of St. Cross, to which is joined The Almshouse of Noble Poverty.

Walking out one afternoon from our oriel-windowed room in the Got Begot Hostel on Winchester's The High, we crossed a grassy meadow watered by the twisting, rapid-flowing brook Itchen. Past Winchester College, the oldest public school in England, and over a turnstile, we came to stately Beaufort Tower and entered a charming Old World community. Its quadrangle looks every bit as old as the eight centuries which have passed since Bishop Henry of Blois established a home for the poor of Christ and set up one of the oldest English benevolent trusts still functioning. He founded St. Cross "to support wholly thirteen poor men, feeble and so reduced in strength that they can with difficulty support themselves with another's aid." In 1151 the enterprise was turned over to the Knights Hospitaler of St. John of Jerusalem, whose experiences in Palestine had fitted them to care for the sick and to indulge their taste for stately architecture. An unusually large number of mason's marks, as well as tiny shells and vines, are carved on stone walls and column bases.

The brothers wear the same style garments their predecessors used for many centuries—long black gowns with square silver crutch crosses on the left breast, and brimmed black tam-o'-shanter hats. When a brother dies his silver cross is placed in his coffin with him, then removed before interment and handed on to the new arrival who will occupy his tall-chimneyed cottage on the quad.

At Porter's Lodge we bought a small silver cross potent such as the brothers wear. And there, too, we saw a cross potent inlaid in the traditional wooden breadboard on which is served the famous "Wayfarer's Dole"—a medieval charity which assures a piece of bread and a small horn of ale to everyone who applies at the gate for food.

Three hundred years after the establishment of St. Cross a second foundation was laid by Cardinal Beaufort. He specified that his Almshouse of Noble Poverty should not be for "the poorest of the poor," as at St. Cross, but for men and women who "had had everything handsome about them" but had "met losses." They were to wear plum-colored gowns and live in three-roomed garden apartments.

The five crosses of the Jerusalem cross appear on the fire buckets in the Refectory, in the Minstrels' Gallery, and on a wall of the Refectory. But the typical cross of St. Cross is the square cross potent; it looms on the reredos of Norman windows in the Lady Chapel of the Hospital of St. Cross and everywhere throughout this Transition Norman church located on a site visited as a "first pilgrim halting-place" when worshipers from the Continent headed for Canterbury. The vestry room of St. Cross claims to have been a chapel of "the blissful, holy martyr" of Chaucer's *Canterbury Tales*.

Most of our English crosses are linked with historic cathedrals and abbeys. One of them was a part of Lincoln Cathedral. It is fashioned from a slender piece of English oak, removed during a restoration and made into a cross. Another, a small brass Glastonbury cross, has to do with the Arthurian tradition of this ruined Abbey. It is inscribed:

> Here lies buried the illustrious King Arthur,
> In the Island of Avalon.

We found it one day in a bookshop near the romantic ruins of Glastonbury whose abbot was Bishop Henry of

Blois, founder of St. Cross. Few churches in England are so rich in legendary lore as Glastonbury. It claims association with both Joseph of Arimathea and King Arthur, "his descendant." Legend says that in *c.* A.D. 31 on an islet in a marsh called Avalon or Island of Apples, the first British Christians led by Joseph of Arimathea built a church of wattles. This was the same Joseph who was present at the Crucifixion. A second church is thought to have been erected to encase the little reed church. If so, both were destroyed in the fire of 1184.

As if these traditions were not enough, it was "proved" that St. Patrick, evangelist, spent his last years in Glastonbury. And later, hard pressed for funds following the fire of 1184, the Abbey made a timely "discovery of the bones of King Arthur and his fair-haired Queen Guinevere" at Glastonbury.

Of course critics looked askance at this evidence of an event not even mentioned in William of Malmesbury's *On the Antiquity of the Church of Glastonbury* in the twelfth century. Moreover, rivalry between Canterbury and Glastonbury could account for any legend which gave prestige to Glastonbury including the discovery of the huge bones of Arthur in a hollow oak, and the cross of lead, which had been buried face down to avoid identification.

Our choicest English cross is the St. Martin's acquired "as we were going to St. Ives"—by bus. A fellow traveler suggested that when we got to St. Ives and Penzance, we would find beautiful crosses of native Cornish stones—lapis, agate, amethyst. The seed was sown. And no sooner had we installed ourselves in an oceanside hotel in this Cornish resort at the southwest tip of England and had relished our share of appetizing fish and chips than we sought out the lapidaries on the boardwalk promenade. Among an array of geological gems from the mines of Cornwall, we found a handsome piece of English silversmith's work—a St. Martin's Celtic cross which had been made for an exhibit. It is as far removed from the crudity of our Damascus specimen as a lovely English garden is from the dusty Street-Called-Straight. Its chief ornament is a beautifully wrought "true vine," winding itself about both arms of the cross, with clusters of grapes, symbol of the Eucharist, conventionalized at the intersection of the two bars to form a cosmic circle of the timeless sun, perfection, immortality.

Our emblem is studded with stones of brilliant white topaz. We needed no hallmark to assure us of its quality. Adorned with products of Cornish mines, it represents that era in John Wesley's life when he rose before dawn to preach in the open air to Cornish miners at Land's End. The beauty of the St. Martin's emblem made us curious about the saint himself. We learned that he was born of pagan parents *c.* A.D. 316; while in his teens he became a candidate for Christian baptism; later reluctantly entered the French army. One night while on duty at Amiens, he was approached by a beggar asking alms. Having no coins, Martin took his sword, divided his cloak and gave half to the old man. That night he dreamed that Christ himself had been disguised as the importunate one. Martin eventually was elected Bishop of Tours, became the patron saint of France, well known for his leniency to the oppressed and for missionary zeal in Brittany.

It seemed fitting that a Cornish silversmith should have designed a St. Martin's cross, for this section of England along the Channel was closely related to the France of the eleventh and fourteenth centuries.

Returning to our hotel we looked across to St. Michael's Mount, a medieval castle-crowned islet offshore, and watched its chapel disappear in the mists and hoped for a morning sun to light the old Celtic cross on the seaward face of the chapel.

One summer several years later, my mother bought a piece which is a worthy companion to the St. Martin's cross. Like this Cornish beauty it is of delicately wrought silver studded with cut amethysts around which winds a delicate vine in which we see both the symbolic branches of the New Testament and also the leaves of the English oak symbolic of virtue and strength. Four well-carved English roses bound the intersection of the arms. Are they Tudor roses, or Christmas roses, or symbols of Christ's martyrdom?

The original St. Martin's cross of Iona stands in front of the Cathedral of the Isles on Iona Island in Argyllshire, fifty miles west of Scotland. This famous center of Celtic Christianity was long sacred because St. Columba of Ireland landed there in 563 and established an influential monastery which attracted spiritual leaders for centuries. Long before Columba came to Iona, the isle had been deemed sacred by Druids whose priests are publicized in the *Commentaries* of Julius Caesar.

The Irish saint Columba was born December 7, 521, in County Donegal. Banishing himself from his homeland, he floated forth perilously in a wicker coracle—a broad boat-basket. One of the fruits of his intense piety was the conversion in northern Scotland through his holy life, his "miracles," sermons, and establishment of monasteries, the most important of which was Iona. Here Columba died while conducting the offices of the Church and was buried here.

Columba inspired the hymn tune, "St. Colomb" by W. S. Hoyte, with words by Frances Havergal, "From Glory unto Glory." He is remembered in the current Iona Movement, led by George McLeod and others who stress the importance of bringing ministers and laymen together in a fellowship of toil—a part of whose fruits has been the restoration of tottering sanctuaries of Iona, aided by funds raised through gifts secured by the Church of Scotland. The Iona Community is doing much to obliterate the damage caused the Holy Isle when the ardor of the Protestant Reformation dismantled the Christian center (1651), long after it had changed over from the Church of Columba and Celtic Christians, to the Church of Rome.

Part of the fame of Iona rests on the number of kings buried there: reputedly forty-eight Scottish kings possibly including Macbeth; eight Danish and Norwegian kings, and one Irish king. Many of the headstones carried crosses, including the one carved on Columba's stone pillow preserved in the Cathedral. There seems to have been an "Appian Way" of crosses leading down to the sea, but during the Reformation the crosses were tossed to the waves.

Iona is the home of four famous Celtic crosses, the most important being the original St. Martin's. This is prized as "one of the most perfect examples of Celtic art in existence." Facing the front of the restored Abbey, it is almost eight feet tall, the broad upright much higher than its transverse, and the intersection crowned with a circle, the Celtic cosmic symbol for the revolving sun, denoting the Resurrection, perfection, timelessness. The face of Iona's St. Martin's cross is carved with figures and what appear to be acorns of immortality. At its center is a circled figure of a seated Christ. Symbolic animals are also incorporated in the design. The silver and topaz-studded St. Martin's cross in our collection is a handsome adaptation of the original.

The second of four Iona crosses is the St. John's whose transverse arm is broader than that of the St. Martin's, and whose decoration includes a centered crown of thorns and the basket-weave or ribbon-weave "endless" designs characteristic of Celtic art. The extant St. John's was restored in 1926 from a tenth-century original.

The third notable Iona cross is the Maclean, a fifteenth-century wayside cross with extremely short transverse arms. Fourth, there is the handsome MacKinnon cross. Other less important Iona crosses include a St. Patrick's cross, influenced by the Celtic art characteristic of his burial place in County Down, Ireland, and several ancient crosses in the Nunnery of the sixteenth-century prioress Anna.

One day in the cathedral town of Canterbury we chanced upon another clue to the influence of Martin upon the sacred iconography of Great Britain. We entered the Cathedral by the South Porch and spent the morning marveling at what we saw in its vast length; climbed the worn steps where Chaucer walked; were deeply impressed by the thirteenth-century glass, older than that of Chartres. In sapphires, rubies, topaz, emeralds, flash colors from a texture so strong that it cannot be cut with a diamond—such glass is one of England's first concerns when "wars and rumors of wars" necessitate the removal of treasures. The Tomb of the Black Prince, St. Augustine's Chair, the Chapel where à Becket was murdered in 1190, the cloister with eight hundred coats of arms many of them cross-emblazoned—all these features of the Cathedral impressed us. But we wanted a cross for our collection.

On altars and walls in the vast Cathedral which ultimately developed (*c.* 950–1174) from Augustine's early basilica, we had been seeing pleasing square crosses with their ends curving to become parts of a bounding circle. We were told that these were consecration crosses, instituted by Emperor Theodosius at Constantinople in the fourth century, to be placed in heathen temples that were about to be made into Christian churches. Justinian's law decreed that no new church was to be begun until a bishop had first made a prayer and affixed the consecration cross in the place where the new church would rise.

Chance led us down a little thoroughfare known as King's Bridge. There, affixed to a charming old house along the tiny canal, we saw a shingle: "Canterbury Weavers' Jewelry Shop." We soon found ourselves inside a house famous because it had been the home of French Huguenots who, fleeing from persecution in France, here set up their silk looms and pursued their arts and crafts. It was crammed with interesting articles. And for us, there was waiting a Canterbury cross, shaped like the consecration crosses we had been seeing all morning in the Cathedral, its square arms extending to form segments of an incomplete but clearly apparent circle. Its details of carved vine are copied from a cross found in St. George Street in 1860. Studded with marcasite and having at its center a topaz, it proved irresistible as an expression of Canterbury's Christian influence.

This famous city has shrines which are even more interesting than the Cathedral—whose proper name is Christ Church, so called by Augustine as he remembered the tall, plain silver cross and the painting of the Saviour he had carried when his band of missionaries sent out by Gregory at Rome landed in Kent on their task of spreading Christianity among the Saxons.

St. Martin's is considered the oldest church in England, having held services for thirteen centuries. It was built by British Christians in Roman times and was used as a private chapel by the pagan King Ethelbert's Christian Queen Bertha, a pious French woman, who, remembering the patron of her French homeland, Martin of Tours, called the chapel St. Martin's and was happy to share it with Augustine and his fellow missionaries. Through their influence, Ethelbert was persuaded to be baptized by immersion in a large font in St. Martin's Church on June 2, 597.

Of great interest are the vestiges of St. Augustine's own Monastery and Abbey Church, where the good Queen Bertha, King Ethelbert, and Augustine were buried—a church once considered more magnificent than the Cathedral. Its ruins took on life for us when we saw them incorporated into St. Augustine's College, where the students in training for the mission service of the Church of England were celebrating their morning communion in their favorite place, a fourteenth-century crypt chapel.

The influence of Celtic iconography is to be seen in the United States, especially in the National Cathedral at St.

Albans, Washington, where an outdoor Celtic cross stands near the main entrance.

Six Celtic crosses of various types are in our collection. Two of them are from Princes Street, Edinburgh; one from Iona; one from Cornwall; two from America. All are of tall, graceful proportions with arms curved at the intersection and bounded by a circle, as in our St. Martin's. All are decorated with runic designs; bosses (small knoblike protuberances) in groups of five to symbolize the five wounds of the Saviour; chainwork; checker patterns; "Solomon's seals" and network such as is seen all through Eastern Christendom and on many a Byzantine, Russian, and Moslem manuscript. But one of our most unusual Celtic crosses is fashioned of black Irish bog oak. Slender angelic figures are carved upon it, radiantly singing.

Very recently another Celtic cross was sent from Edinburgh's Princes Street by a devout Christian lady. The National Museum of Antiquities of Scotland identified this superb piece of heavy silver as a Kildalton cross, "one of the few Scottish examples of free-standing crosses of Irish type. It is decorated with bosses in Pictish style. The Viking raiders seem to have ended this art-form." Our Kildalton specimen is a Calvary type, having three steps symbolic of faith, hope, love. The intersection of its arms—the upright being one and one-half times taller than the transverse is broad— is bounded by the cosmic circle of "unendingness." Obverse and reverse are carefully carved with the symbolic winged man, Matthew; winged lion, Mark; winged ox, Luke; and the eagle, John. Lower portions of the upright carry winged creatures and scrollwork typical of Celtic art.

❧ 12 ❧

Nestorian Crosses

WITH SYMBOLS, as with people, mistaken identities sometimes develop. This happened in the case of the innocent hoax concerning the origin of so-called early first-century crosses marked in charcoal on stone ossuaries (bone chests) discovered at Talpiyoth along the road between Jerusalem and Bethlehem. These crosses were publicized in articles which appeared over the signature of an established expert on Palestinian ossuaries and tombs. Effort was made to establish the fact that the cross was used as a Christian symbol in Jerusalem before A.D. 71. The ossuaries were dated first century by a pottery jug and coins of A.D. 42–43 during the reign of Agrippa I. One repository, cross-marked, was believed to hold the remains of a Jewish family whose members had been disciples of Jesus. The square charcoal marks are accompanied by words interpreted as "Jesus woe," or "Jesus Aloth." Yet "Jesus Aloth" might be the name of the family, members of which had been buried near by, and their disintegrated bones later placed in the ossuary. Dr. Karl H. Kraeling, Director of the Oriental Institute, discredited the crosses. He thought they were probably nothing more than space-filling designs, or signs that the box was full, or charms to ward off evil spirits, rather than Christian crosses on the tomb of witnesses of the crucifixion of Jesus. Crossed lines were often used by masons, for one purpose or another—as the square ones painted on the Egyptian Solar Ship of Cheops.

A study of Nestorian crosses raises many questions concerning mistaken identity. In an earlier book on crosses we mentioned our Nestorian cross. This small bronze emblem may indeed be twelve hundred years old, as a Chinese Christian educator from Hiroshima dated it. It came into our possession years ago from the large collection of Nestorian crosses gathered by the late Dr. Mark Brown, an American Methodist missionary, and was regarded by him as a cross of the type which had been scattered by Nestorian Christians through West China's Ordos loop of the Yellow River. Their emphasis was upon the dual nature of Christ, as opposed to the tenet of the Monophysites.

The leader of this movement, Nestorius, was born in Germanicia at the foot of the Taurus Mountains, whose cold waters cascaded to the plain of Tarsus, birthplace of Paul. After his education in Antioch, and his service as a monk and presbyter, this eloquent orthodox ascetic was elevated to the patriarchate of Constantinople, where he was consecrated April 10, 428. When Nestorius attacked the current custom of calling Mary the mother of Jesus also "Mother of God," his opponents at Constantinople complained to Pope Celestine I. Nestorius was hailed before a council called at Ephesus in 431, and without being heard was deposed. In modern times, the thinking of Nestorius has become available through his letters and data in Syrian manuscripts.

Nestorian Christianity made its way into China about A.D. 636, either by a long trek through Central Asia or by ship from India. The brilliant Tang Dynasty (A.D. 618–906) welcomed the new faith. Again a few centuries later it enjoyed a revival under the Yuan Dynasty. Evidences of Nestorian churches have been found as far west as Szechuan.

Marco Polo, in his famous narrative dictated in a Genoese prison from notebooks he had made in China, says that he found so many Nestorians living side by side with Moslems, under the tolerance of the great Jenghiz Khan, that there were as many as three churches in one town. In Tenduk, an eastern province, he found Christian rulers with their Christian subjects earning their living by weaving the fine silks and gold tissues ornamented with pearl for which Chinese have long been noted. He reported that "Christian carpenters and smiths were able workmen." The great Jenghiz Khan gave his son in marriage to a Christian princess; in fact, Christian wives seem to have been preferred for royal sons.

Today few traces of true Nestorian crosses are found in China, other than the famous Nestorian Stele, a ten-foot-high tablet at Sianfu, Shensi, which incorporates a small Christian cross. This monument dates from A.D. 779 or 781 and carries inscriptions in Chinese and in Syriac, stating doctrines of Nestorian Christians, and records the coming of A-lo-pên, a Syrian monk, to this region in 635. It mentions a personal God as a source of the Universe, tells of man's Creation and Fall; of the Incarnation and the redemptive mission of Christ. The inscription also records later experiences of

Nestorians, praises the co-operation of emperors and of the Nestorian patron, 'Shu, to whom the tablet may have been dedicated.

The Nestorian cross at Sianfu is basically square; its arms taper gracefully toward the intersection; and each arm terminates in three pearl-like rings denoting the Trinity. Upholding the cross is a flying cloud, symbol of immortality among Chinese Taoists and Buddhists. Below the cloud is the lotus, Buddhist symbol. Such syncretism may account for the disappearance of Nestorians in China.

An ecumenical adaptation of the original Sianfu Nestorian cross was achieved by a Christian Iranian painter, Hosein Behzad-Miniateur, in a silver plaque presented to the Board of Foreign Missions of the Presbyterian Church, U.S.A., by the Church of Christ in Iran.

A former postal commissioner of Peiping, F. A. Nixon, has a group of several hundred Nestorian pieces which may be the world's largest collection of Nestorian symbols. Details carved on such enigmatic bronze crosses seem to include concentric circles, a trinitarian symbol in some parts of the Christian world; anchors, lighthouses, iotas, conventionalized birds and fishes, a chalice design, elements of the Christian monogram; a Theta (Greek letter Θ denoting *Theos*, God).

Nestorians usually forbade the use of the crucifix as representational art in their worship, using only the cross and portraits of Christ in their churches. In view of the gross idols worshiped by the pagan Chinese whom they hoped to win, this was a necessary strategy, as well as a part of their basic belief that the cross itself stands for Christ.

The cross in our collection which we classify as Nestorian

is a square, openwork Maltese type, measuring about two inches. In addition to the swastika at the center other symbols include in each arm a T-shaped design which may be a Greek letter T or may be a Tau cross. Each T-shaped cross rests upon a segment of a circle, immortality, which bounds an inner cross with equal arms tapering toward the center. There is evidence that this was a "body cross" attached to a leather thong by a wide loop on its reverse side. So steadily was it worn for generations that the bronze loop is thinned to a mere thread. Owners may never have known the meaning of the symbols but valued them as protective amulets. Some scholars believe the crosses were symbolic seals, used to stamp lumps of mud placed on locks of primitive homes when owners went away. One theory is that the worn-looped emblems were used to stamp wafers for the church.

After studying our Nestorian crosses Dr. Schuyler Van R. Cammann of the University Museum, University of Pennsylvania, long interested in Christian symbolism of the Far East, believes that it represents in every detail the old pagan Asian concept of the cosmos. He finds nothing distinctively Christian in it. In Asia the cross was a symbol of magic, of temporal and spiritual dominion, and of power. In pre-Christian times Asians cast or carved their idea of the universe, usually based on a cross-shaped diagram representing the four directions and having at the center a square or a circle with a sun symbol, as the swastika. As to the first crucifixes of Christendom, Dr. Cammann believes that perhaps these may have been intended to denote *Christus Rex* and that the cross may have been originally intended as a symbol of his dominion over "all the world."

Dr. John S. Thatcher of Dumbarton Oaks Research Library suggests that Nestorian crosses like our specimen may be pre-Christian seals. But Professor J. M. Menzies, formerly of Cheloo University, believes them to be surely of Christian origin.

So the debate concerning the identity of the Nestorian crosses continues. Although not definitely established, there is circumstantial evidence to identify them as "the property of Mongol Nestorian Christians in northwest China in the thirteenth century, to which Chinese experts in bronze date them."

≥13≤

American Crosses

THE USE OF Christian symbolism is to be found in a large proportion of churches in the United States. The Puritan Founding Fathers bequeathed a Protestant church which was devoid of beauty, but the years have softened their influence and religious art has won its way. The cross, once considered a Roman Catholic symbol, is ubiquitous as the central symbol of Christianity.

Frequent reference has been made to three collections of valuable ancient crosses: Byzantine specimens at Dumbarton Oaks Research Library; The Cloisters, including its Treasury; and the Metropolitan Museum of Art in New York. In the latter a recent acquisition is a notable tall processional cross which greatly enriches our knowledge of liturgical silver designed for public use.

This rare piece of Christian symbolic art was made of thin sheets of silver mounted on a wooden core which disintegrated through the centuries, but has since been skillfully replaced by a French art firm. In between fragments of the initial material, plaster applied to the wood gives the appearance of the original metal. The very slender proportions of this cross, which is somewhat Roman in shape, are given grace by a broadening out at the ends of the four arms. It bears an inscription in Greek, indicating that it had been presented to a church by some unnamed donor, for the salvation or the repose of two men, Herodotus and Komitas. Its front is inscribed with the important invocation famous in Byzantine liturgy, "Holy God, Holy Mighty One, Holy Immortal One, have mercy on us." This Trisagion, carried from Syria to Gaul, became incorporated in the Mass as an introductory section. On Good Friday it is repeated in Greek and Latin. This cross helps us envision the role of processions in the early centuries of the Christian Church. Reproductions of its type are effective when hung against textile reredos above altars in deep chancels.

Other beautifully proportioned sixth-century Syrian crosses are displayed in the same gallery. From the fourth and fifth centuries is a cross used with other symbols on an Early Christian bottle of uncolored glass; a gracefully proportioned, tall gold cross in the bottom of a fragment of a bowl; one squarish cross; and two lamps, whose handles are in the form of a cross. One gold cross, which is part of a sixth-century Byzantine necklace, is of exquisite proportions. The Byzantine enamels, made in the imperial workshop between the eighth and twelfth centuries, constitute the most comprehensive collection extant.

Our collection is enriched by a cross made by an old American seaman a century or more ago. His ship perished on a Maine reef, and he with it. But in his mariner's trunk was found testimony to the eternal yearning in the heart of man to express himself in worshipful beauty, though the worshiper may be chronically out of touch with the church. The mariner perhaps never heard William Whiting's hymn, but he must have experienced its poignant entreaty:

> Eternal Father, strong to save
>
> .   .   .   .
>
> Hear us when we cry to Thee
> For those in peril on the sea.

From fragments of stray wood on his cargo ship this Yankee salt had fashioned a well-proportioned cross about six inches high, with an oblique transverse bar. After painting it a delicate sea green he had paved it skillfully with tiny seashells, and at the center he had cemented a little five-pointed starfish, placing Bethlehem thus at the heart of Calvary, as the designer of our elaborate gold Russian cross placed the star at the center of his cross. The old sailor had wrought a symbolic hill of Golgotha from a rounded, skull-like shell from which his cross rises. Near that lowest shell he had fastened bits of purple-red sea moss to indicate the redeeming blood of his Lord. Our whole collection has no more adequate or moving symbol than this designed by the hands of a forgotten mariner. The roar of the sea is in this cross. It speaks to us of the God who made heaven and earth, the sea and "all that in them is." And it speaks to us of the courageous men who sail for the benefit of humanity:

> Some went down to the sea in ships,
>   doing business on the great waters;
> they saw the deeds of the Lord
>   his wondrous works in the deep.
>   PSALM 107:23–24

An American marine cross was designed by William W. Edel while serving as chaplain at Sampson Naval Training Station on Lake Champlain. We prize the specimen in our collection. This symbol has taken its place in American iconographic art. It applies a stark Latin cross in bold relief against a background of the mariner's compass which serves as an aureole for the cross, or as a sunburst symbolic of immortality. The compass denotes that the cross has power to help life's mariners find their way under every situation. Speaking of his mariner's cross, the designer remarked, "For me it symbolizes the dependence which seamen must ever place upon the Pilot of Galilee, who alone can guide them safely through the storms of life."

An appropriate companion to the marine cross is one fashioned from a scrap of plexiglass which was part of an airplane that flew over Japan during World War II.

A cross linked with early colonial history is the oak cross made from wood taken from Old St. John's Church at Richmond, Virginia, where in 1775 the young American patriot, Patrick Henry, rose in a convention being held in this church to protest against the oppressive measures of the British. "Is life so dear or peace so sweet as to be purchased at the price of chains and slavery? Forbid it, Almighty God! I know not what course others may take, but as for me, give me liberty or give me death!" A challenge still, after two centuries, to oppressed minorities everywhere!

No group of American crosses would be complete without an American Indian cross. One came into our collection in an unexpected way which illustrates how collectors become detectives, piecing together bits of apparently unrelated information. Following a lecture on the cross, I received a letter containing pictures of three Indian crosses which had been dug up a half century earlier near the site of Fort Ouiatenon, on the banks of the Wabash near Lafayette, Indiana. This fort stood near a group of Indian villages which formed the largest Indian settlement in the Middle West. It saw stormy scenes for seventy years until destroyed during the time of General George Washington.

These crosses suggest more than the conflict between French traders, English soldiers, and Colonial regiments. They indicate the missionary efforts of the French Jesuits who for many years influenced North American aborigines away from their worship of wooden idols, feather-trimmed gods, and nature elements to a clearer knowledge of the Great Spirit. These silver crosses probably belonged to Jesuits near Fort Ouiatenon or to their Indian converts whose presence at this western fort is attested by two baptismal records housed in the cathedral at Vincennes, Indiana.

We filed the picture of those two-century-old silver Lorraine crosses, and hoped that sometime an American Indian cross might find its way into our collection. One Christmas a friend came to our home saying, "Yesterday I was looking about in a dusty shop. Something led me to inquire if its piles of junk might yield some sort of cross. See what I discovered!"

Opening the Christmas package, I found what looked to be a counterpart of the old Lorraine silver cross which had long lain pictured in our files.

The American southwest furnished two other crosses for our collection: one, a modern Indian's handiwork in silver carved with stars, sun, and symbolic mountains; the other, a stately silver Latin cross paved with rose mineral from Taxco, Mexico. Pittsburgh provided our collection with an elegant cross of coppery green malachite, gold-mounted. It had been part of the Andrew Mellon estate.

Another American cross we call our "benediction cross," because on its plain old silver face there is carved the Old Testament word of blessing, "Mizpah." And then there is that almost invisible cross, brought one day by a very humble friend ambitious of contributing the "smallest of all" to our collection. And she did. It measures one quarter of an inch. And there is one brought by another friend, which she asked us to call our cross from "where cross the crowded ways of life" because she had bought it at the crossroads of Manhattan— Fifth Avenue and Forty-second Street.

Latin American crosses were developed from Spanish and Portuguese originals, although sometimes slightly redesigned and often encrusted with inappropriately costly jewels. Central America is represented in our collection by a colorful coral-studded Panamanian cross of solid gold, whose hue recalls the desire for gold which lured early explorers and exploiters.

Canadian American crosses have baffled us. In Quebec, so full of artistic vestiges of the old French colonial days, we came off defeated. At Sainte Anne de Beaupré and at Montreal we found only modern crosses.

The Canadian cross we remember most vividly is the one at Grand Pré in Nova Scotia. There, near the site of the little French country chapel where Longfellow's Evangeline and her French Norman townsfolk worshiped before their deportation by the English in 1755, is a stout peasant cross made of stones picked from ruined farmhouses of this industrious people. On the site from which the brokenhearted group were launched into unknown destinies, another cross of simple metal has been erected—a French cross with trefoil ends, its circle of immortality pierced by four spears. And on the chapel which replaces the one the Acadians knew is a slender spire topped by a distinctive French Norman cross. The Grand Pré crosses are symbolic of that host of transferred populations seen in many parts of the world in our own century.

➤ 14 ➤

Beyond the Cross

AT SOME TIME in the life of every person the cross becomes an experience. It is no longer a symbol, beautifully jeweled and shot through with light rays. When once accepted, it is the Light itself.

Just as our collection of crosses began unexpectedly on that happy morning in Athens, so it closed with Lane's return from his last journey to the lands of the cross—the only one I had not been able to share. When his graceful ship eased herself to anchor in the North River, he was standing on the sun deck signaling that he would soon come ashore. In his new French-blue duffel bag of gifts there was a package containing twelve more crosses he had assembled from various countries. Strange, that there should have been exactly *twelve*.

For a few months we enjoyed these together. We had no misgivings such as Edna St. Vincent Millay expressed in *Mine the Harvest:*

Those hours when happy hours were my estate,
Entailed, as proper, for the next in line,

169

Yet mine the harvest, and the title mine—
Those acres, fertile, and the furrow straight,
From which the lark would rise—all of my late
Enchantments, still, in brilliant colours, shine,
But striped with black, the tulip, lawn and vine,
Like gardens looked at through an iron gate.

Yet not as one who never sojourned there
I view the lovely segments of a past.
I lived with all my senses, well aware
That this was perfect, and it would not last;
I smell the flower, though vacuum-still the air;
I feel its texture, though the gate is fast.

Life had given us some crosses to carry. Always, God had given us strength to lift them, together. But one evening something happened that we could do nothing about.

The heaviest cross ever laid upon me was the loss of my husband whose creative powers had made so much of my life beautiful. The night of his death, as I returned from the hospital in the winter foredawn whose darkness seemed momentarily the only symbol I could understand, I passed our church. The bulletin board read:

Don't be Afraid of Tomorrow—
God is Already There.

I accepted this truth. Once back home I went to one of the long French windows of the old parsonage living room and looked out onto the winter-frozen garden, where the pale January sun was already piercing the pine grove. It occurred to me then that there is no interim between life and death. Both are parts of one process. Just as a baby's first

act is to respire, to take his initial breath, so a man's last act
is to expire, to breathe his last breath.

But soon after I had yielded to inexorable fact, the spiritual, well-known personality began manifesting himself to
me. He has never ceased to do so. Not long after his passing,
I wrote these lines. They have strengthened me ever since.

TODAY . . . PARADISE

There is no interim.
For Love's last breath upon this earth
Is his first breath in that new birth
That makes of him
A strong young creature in Eternity,
Where he is signaling to me,
"Good cheer! Much better to be here.
Take courage. I am always near."

A year or so later my feeling that there is no interim between the ebbing of this world's life and the rising to the
full tide of God's endless life came with new force. I was
reading *The Passion of the King* by Frederick G. Grant: "If
God admits you to fellowship with himself—then the life
to come, which is only the continuance of the fellowship
already established here, is just as natural and inevitable as
the radiation of light or the continuance of the seasons or
the survival of living species upon the earth."

Many, in their progress through the door of the cross, have
had intimations of life persisting in an unseen room.

If the door of the cross closes on a familiar room it also
opens out, wide, into another room which we cannot quite
see. To be sure, the room on which the door closes is filled
with the old familiar precious things that help to make a

home. For me the dear familiar room is filled with furniture bought in early years: the family round table, about which so many significant events took place; rugs bought in colorful Near Eastern bazaars; pottery from the Via Dolorosa; heart-warming paintings from the Balkans. And there, too, is an icon of Jesus, whose calm, majestic, bearded face looks out from its frame of polished brass incorporating a cross-crowned, cloud-borne world resting on the heart of the Saviour.

Of the room into which the door opens, little is known, except that it is spacious enough to hold all the righteous who have ever lived. It is part of the Father's many-roomed mansion, and Christ himself is "the Way," the corridor by which all must eventually come.

The assurance that death is not a final separation was expressed a generation ago on the headstone of two great astronomers, John and Phoebe Brashear, of the Allegheny Observatory, Pittsburgh, Pennsylvania: "We have watched the stars too long together, to be afraid of the night."

Canon Edward N. West in his *Meditations on the Gospel of St. John* says, "It is only because Jesus is ascending to the Father that he can hereafter be with Mary always. After the Ascension, there is no more separation again forever."

At first, I felt that death is permanent. But now I know that death itself is not lasting. Life is the unlasting; immortality the lasting. I felt this assurance in the cemetery when a brown thrush—Lane's favorite—flashed its vibrant wings across my path. I feel it whenever a cardinal with cheerful insistence flings out his summer notes. "He is risen, he is not here." Death's terror is gone, somewhere out there beyond the cross.

Meantime, I have learned the secret of R. H. Granville's "Thrush in a Lonely Field":

> you with your clear tone,
> Piped to a wilderness, have made it clear,
> Love is not love that dare not walk alone.

After a year of new acquaintance with the cross I saw it in a fresh light. One rugged March day while out walking I looked at the cross which tops the belfry of our church. The whole world seemed torn apart by boisterous winds. Masses of gigantic gray clouds were churning and whirling about the cross. At that moment I realized that the cross is the axis on which the force and energy of the universe turn. The cosmos revolves around the cross.

Jerusalem gave us crosses—three of them: two for malefactors, one for the Saviour of the world.

Jerusalem also gave us gardens—three of them claiming to be Gethsemane: Latin, Russian, Armenian-Greek.

But Jerusalem gave us only one inexplicably opened tomb in a hillside cave on Easter morning.

In this lies our only guarantee that "because he lives, we, too, shall live."

The cross of Christ is creative, redemptive, ultimate.

PART II

An Anthology of the Cross

⤟⤠

✄ References to the Cross in Scripture

EXCEPT FOR THE seven last words, immediately following, the Scripture references are listed in the order of their appearance in the books of the New Testament, and are from the Revised Standard Version.

THE SEVEN LAST WORDS FROM THE CROSS

1. Father, forgive them; for they know not what they do. LUKE 23:34

2. Truly, I say to you, today you will be with me in Paradise. LUKE 23:43

3. Woman, behold your son! . . . Behold your mother! JOHN 19:26, 27

4. "Eloi, Eloi, lama sabach-thani?" which means, "My God, my God, why hast thou forsaken me?" MARK 15:34; cf. MATT. 27:46

5. I thirst. JOHN 19:28

6. It is finished. JOHN 19:30

7. Father, into thy hands I commit my spirit! LUKE 23:46

Note that of these seven words, three are addressed directly to God (1, 4, 7); one to the penitent thief (2); one to his mother and his best friend, John (3); two are ultimate statements, addressed to no one (5, 6), and recorded only by John, who was standing close to the cross.

Reviling words were spoken to Jesus by chief priests, scribes, elders (MATT. 27:41 ff.) and by the robbers who were crucified with him (MATT. 27:44).

A commendatory word was spoken about Jesus by one thief, "This man has done nothing wrong. . . . Jesus, remember me when you come into your kingly power" (LUKE 23:41 f.), and by the Roman centurion who was "keeping watch over Jesus"; "Truly this was a son of God!" (MATT. 27:54).

The ultimate word stating the resurrection of Jesus, was spoken by "a young man sitting on the right side [of the tomb], dressed in a white robe. . . . 'He has risen, he is not here. . . . he is going before you to Galilee; there you will see him, as he told you.'" MARK 16:5 ff.

. . . he who does not take his cross and follow me is not worthy of me. MATT. 10:38; cf. MARK 8:34, LUKE 14:27

If any man would come after me, let him deny himself and take up his cross and follow me. MATT. 16:24; cf. LUKE 9:23, "take up his cross daily."

As they were marching out, they came upon a man of Cyrene, Simon by name; this man they compelled to carry his cross. MATT. 27:32; cf. MARK 15:21, LUKE 23:26, "carry it behind Jesus."

If you are the Son of God, come down from the cross. MATT. 27:40; cf. MARK 15:30

He is the King of Israel; let him come down now from the cross, and we will believe in him. MATT. 27:42; cf. MARK 15:32

I, when I am lifted up from the earth, will draw all men to myself. JOHN 12:32

So they took Jesus, and he went out, bearing his own cross, to the place called the place of a skull, which is called in Hebrew Golgotha. There they crucified him, and with him two others, one on either side, and Jesus between them. JOHN 19:17 f.

Pilate also wrote a title and put it on the cross; it read, "Jesus of Nazareth, the King of the Jews." JOHN 19:19

. . . but standing by the cross of Jesus were his mother, and his mother's sister, Mary the wife of Clopas, and Mary Magdalene. JOHN 19:25

Since it was the day of Preparation, in order to prevent the bodies from remaining on the cross on the sabbath (for that sabbath was a high day), the Jews asked Pilate that their legs might be broken, and that they might be taken away. JOHN 19:31

For Christ did not send me to baptize but to preach the gospel, and not with eloquent wisdom, lest the cross of Christ be emptied of its power. For the word of the cross is folly to those who are perishing, but to us who are being saved it is the power of God. I COR. 1:17 f.

. . . the stumbling-block of the cross has been removed. GAL. 5:11

And those who belong to Christ Jesus have crucified the flesh with its passions and desires. GAL. 5:24

. . . in order that they may not be persecuted for the cross of Christ. GAL. 6:12

But far be it from me to glory except in the cross of our Lord Jesus Christ, by which the world has been crucified to me, and I to the world. GAL. 6:14

Henceforth let no man trouble me; for I bear on my body the marks of Jesus. GAL. 6:17

. . . and might reconcile us both to God in one body through the cross, thereby bringing the hostility to an end. EPHES. 2:16

And being found in human form he humbled himself and became obedient unto death, even death on a cross. PHIL. 2:8

For many, of whom I have often told you and now tell you even with tears, live as enemies of the cross of Christ. PHIL. 3:18

For in him all the fullness of God was pleased to dwell, and through him to reconcile to himself all things, whether on earth or in heaven, making peace by the blood of his cross. COL. 1:19 f.

. . . having canceled the bond which stood against us with its legal demands; this he set aside, nailing it to the cross. COL. 2:14

Therefore, since we are surrounded by so great a cloud of witnesses, let us also lay aside every weight, and sin which clings so closely, and let us run with perserverance the race that is set before us, looking to Jesus the pioneer and perfecter of our faith, who for the joy that was set before him endured the cross, despising the shame, and is seated at the right hand of the throne of God. HEB. 12:1 f.

. . . and their dead bodies will lie in the street of the great city which is allegorically called Sodom and Egypt, where their Lord was crucified. REV. 11:8

THE CRUCIFIXION, IN SCRIPTURE

Behold, we are going up to Jerusalem; and the Son of man will be delivered to the chief priests and scribes, and they will condemn him to death, and deliver him to the Gentiles to be mocked and scourged and crucified. MATT. 20:18 f.

Therefore I send you prophets and wise men and scribes, some of whom you will kill and crucify. MATT. 23:34

You know that after two days the Passover is coming, and the Son of man will be delivered up to be crucified. MATT. 26:2

Pilate said to them, "Then what shall I do with Jesus who is called Christ?" They all said, "Let him be crucified." MATT. 27:22; cf. JOHN 19:15

But they shouted all the more, "Let him be crucified." MATT. 27:23

. . . scourged Jesus, delivered him to be crucified. MATT. 27:26

And when they had crucified him, they divided his garments among them by casting lots. MATT. 27:35

Then two robbers were crucified with him, one on the right and one on the left. MATT. 27:38.

But the angel said to the women, "Do not be afraid; for I know that you seek Jesus who was crucified." MATT. 28:5

Do not be amazed; you seek Jesus of Nazareth, who was crucified. MARK 16:6

And when they came to the place which is called The Skull, there they crucified him, and the criminals. LUKE 23:33

. . . our chief priests and rulers delivered him up to be condemned to death, and crucified him. LUKE 24:20

". . . and I, when I am lifted up from the earth, will draw all men to myself." He said this to show by what death he was to die. JOHN 12:32 f.

Now in the place where he was crucified there was a garden, and in the garden a new tomb where no one had ever been laid . . . they laid Jesus there. JOHN 19:41 f.

Let all the house of Israel therefore know assuredly that God has made him both Lord and Christ, this Jesus whom you crucified. ACTS 2:36; from an address of Peter at Jerusalem

. . . be it known to you all, and to all the people of Israel, that by the name of Jesus Christ of Nazareth, whom you crucified, whom God raised from the dead, by him this man is standing by you well. ACTS 4:10

We know that our old self was crucified with him so that the sinful body might be destroyed. ROM. 6:6

Was Paul crucified for you? I COR. 1:13

. . . we preach Christ crucified, . . . Christ the power of God and the wisdom of God. I COR. 1:23 f.

When I came to you, brethren, I did not come proclaiming to you the testimony of God in lofty words or wisdom. For I decided to know nothing among you except Jesus Christ and him crucified. I COR. 2:1

None of the rulers of this age understood this; for if they had, they would not have crucified the Lord of glory. I COR. 2:8

For he was crucified in weakness, but lives by the power of God. II COR. 13:4

I have been crucified with Christ; it is no longer I who live, but Christ who lives in me; and the life I now live in the flesh I live by faith in the Son of God, who loved me and gave himself for me. GAL. 2:20

. . . they crucify the Son of God on their own account and hold him up to contempt. HEB. 6:6

TREE, IN SENSE OF CROSS

The God of our fathers raised Jesus whom you killed by hanging him on a tree. ACTS 5:30

And we are witnesses to all that he did both in the country of the Jews and in Jerusalem. They put him to death by hanging him on a tree. ACTS 10:39

And when they had fulfilled all that was written of him, they took him down from the tree, and laid him in a tomb. ACTS 13:29

Christ redeemed us from the curse of the law, having become a curse for us—for it is written, "Cursed be every one who hangs on a tree." GAL. 3:13

He himself bore our sins in his body on the tree, that we might die to sin and live to righteousness. By his wounds you have been healed. I PETER 2:24

Hymns of the Cross

SOME of the hymns listed below deal in their entirety with the theme of the Cross; other hymns refer to the cross in one or more stanzas.

Abide with me, HENRY F. LYTE

Above the hills of time the Cross is gleaming,
THOMAS TIPLADY

Alas! and did my Saviour bleed? ISAAC WATTS

Alleluia! Alleluia! Alleluia! GIOVANNI P. DA PALESTRINA

Am I a soldier of the cross? ISAAC WATTS

"Are ye able?" said the Master, EARL MARLATT

Ask ye what great thing I know? JOHANN C. SCHWENDLER

Before the cross of Jesus, FERDINAND Q. BLANCHARD

Beneath the cross of Jesus, ELIZABETH C. CLEPHANE

Christ our Lord is risen to-day, CHARLES WESLEY

Come to Calvary's holy mountain, JAMES MONTGOMERY

Dey crucified my Lord, NEGRO SPIRITUAL

Discipleship, S. RALPH HARLOW

Fling out the banner, GEORGE W. DOANE

Go to dark Gethsemane, JAMES MONTGOMERY

Hope of the World, GEORGIA HARKNESS

In the cross of Christ I glory, JOHN BOWRING

In the hour of trial, JAMES MONTGOMERY

Jesus, and shall it ever be? Joseph Grigg
Jesus, keep me near the cross, Fanny J. Crosby
Jesus spreads his banner o'er us, Roswell Park
Lead on, O King eternal, Ernest W. Shurtleff
Look, ye saints, the sight is glorious, Thomas Kelly
Love divine, what hast thou done! Charles Wesley
Must Jesus bear the cross alone? Thomas Shepherd
Near the cross was Mary weeping, Jacopone Da Todi
tr. James W. Alexander
Never further than Thy cross, Elizabeth R. Charles
O come and mourn with me awhile, Frederick W. Faber
O Jesus, thou art standing, William W. How
O Love divine, what hast thou done! Charles Wesley
O Love that wilt not let me go, George Matheson
Onward, Christian soldiers, Sabine Baring-Gould
O sacred Head, now wounded, St. Bernard of Clairvaux,
Paul Gerhardt, tr. by James W. Alexander
O young and fearless Prophet, S. Ralph Harlow
Rejoice, ye pure in heart! Edward H. Plumptre
Rise up, O men of God, William P. Merrill
Rock of ages, cleft for me, Augustus M. Toplady
Saviour, thy dying love, Sylvanus D. Phelps
Saviour, when in dust, to thee, Robert Grant
Spirit of God! descend upon my heart, George Croly
There is a fountain filled with blood, Thomas Cowper
There is a green hill far away, Cecil F. Alexander
The King of love my Shepherd is, Henry W. Baker
The old rugged cross, George Bennard
The Son of God goes forth to war, Reginald Heber
Thou didst leave thy throne, Emily E. S. Elliott

Through the night of doubt and sorrow,
        BERNHARDT S. INGEMANN, tr. by SABINE BARING-GOULD
"'Tis finished!" so the Saviour cried, SAMUEL STENNETT
Were you there when they crucified my Lord?
                                            NEGRO SPIRITUAL
When I survey the wondrous cross, ISAAC WATTS

Poems about the Cross and the Crucifixion of Christ

CRUCIFIXION

Lord, must I bear the whole of it, or none?
"Even as I was crucified, My son."

Will it suffice if I the thorn-crown wear?
"To take the scourge, My shoulders were made bare."

My hands, O Lord, must I be pierced in both?
"Twain gave I to the hammer, nothing loath."

But surely, Lord, my feet need not be nailed?
"Had Mine not been, then love had not prevailed."

What need I more, O Lord, to fill my part?
"Only the spear-point in thy broken heart."

Frederick George Scott

A BALLAD OF TREES AND THE MASTER

Into the woods my Master went,
Clean forspent, forspent.

Into the woods my Master came,
Forspent with love and shame.
But the olives they were not blind to Him;
The little grey leaves were kind to Him;
The thorn-tree had a mind to Him
When into the woods He came.

Out of the woods my Master went,
And He was well content.
Out of the woods my Master came,
Content with death and shame.
When Death and Shame would woo Him last,
From under the trees they drew Him last:
'Twas on a tree they slew Him—last:
When out of the woods He came.

Sidney Lanier

THEN—AND NOW

THEN!—Crowned with the thorn,
      He died
      The death of scorn—
      The Crucified!
NOW! —THINE IS THE KINGDOM
      And THE POWER, and THE GLORY,
      FOR EVER and FOR EVER.

John Oxenham

LIVE CHRIST

Live Christ!—and though thy life may be
In much a valedictory,

The heavy cross brings seeming loss,
But wins the crown of victory.

John Oxenham

THE CROSS AT THE CROSSWAYS

See there! God's signpost, standing at the ways
　　Which every man of his free will must go—
Up the steep hill, or down the winding ways,
　　One or the other, every man must go.

He forces no man, each must choose his way,
　　And as he chooses, so the end will be;
One went in front to point the Perfect Way,
　　Who follows fears not where the end will be.

John Oxenham

From THE EVERLASTING MERCY

"Saul Kane," she said, "when next you drink,
　　Do me the gentleness to think
　　That every drop of drink accursed
　　Makes Christ within you die of thirst,
　　That every dirty word you say
　　Is one more flint upon His way,
　　Another thorn about His head,
　　Another mock by where He tread,
　　Another nail, another cross.
　　All that you are is that Christ's loss."

John Masefield

INDIFFERENCE

When Jesus came to Golgotha they hanged Him on a tree,
They drave great nails through hands and feet, and made a
    Calvary;
They crowned Him with a crown of thorns, red were His
    wounds and deep,
For those were crude and cruel days, the human flesh was
    cheap.

When Jesus came to Birmingham, they simply passed Him by,
They never hurt a hair of Him, they only let Him die;
For men had grown more tender, and they would not give
    Him pain,
They only just passed down the street, and left Him in the
    rain.

Still Jesus cried, "Forgive them, for they know not what
    they do,"
And still it rained the winter rain that drenched Him through
    and through;
The crowds went home and left the streets without a soul
    to see,
And Jesus crouched against a wall and cried for Calvary.

                           G. A. Studdert-Kennedy

CALVARY

Friendless and faint, with martyred steps and slow,
Faint for the flesh, but for the spirit free,
Stung by the mob that came to see the show,
The Master toiled along to Calvary;

We gibed him as he went, with houndish glee,
Till his dimmed eyes for us did overflow;
We cursed his vengeless hand thrice wretchedly—
And this was nineteen hundred years ago.

But after nineteen hundred years the shame
Still clings, and we have not made good the loss
That outraged faith had entered in his name.
Ah, when shall come love's courage to be strong!
Tell me, O Lord, tell me, O Lord, how long
Are we to keep Christ writhing on the cross!

                                 Edwin Arlington Robinson

IN FLANDERS FIELDS

In Flanders fields the poppies blow
Between the crosses, row on row,
        That mark our place; and in the sky
        The larks, still bravely singing, fly,
Scarce heard amid the guns below.

We are the Dead. Short days ago
We lived, felt the dawn, saw sunset glow,
        Loved and were loved, and now we lie
        In Flanders fields.

Take up our quarrel with the foe;
To you from falling hands we throw
        The torch; be yours to hold it high!
        If ye break faith with us who die
We shall not sleep, though poppies grow
        In Flanders fields.

                                 John McCrae

O CONSTANT CROSS

"O Constant cross,
    Would I might put you down," I said
"The road I walk so burdened
    Lies so beautiful, ahead!

"Without you, I'd go proudly,
    Without you, I might run,
Here on the loveliest road of all,
    Straight toward the sun."

A voice spoke from the cross,
    And light became my load:
"Save that you bore me bravely,
    You had not found the road."

                          Violet Alleyn Storey

PRAYER IN AFFLICTION

Keep me from bitterness. It is so easy
To nurse sharp bitter thoughts each dull dark hour.
Against self-pity, Man of Sorrows, defend me,
With Thy deep sweetness and Thy gentle power.
And out of all this hurt of pain and heartbreak
Help me to harvest a new sympathy
For suffering human kind; a wiser pity
For those who lift a heavier cross with Thee.

                          Violet Alleyn Storey

I SEE HIS BLOOD UPON THE ROSE

I see his blood upon the rose
And in the stars the glory of his eyes,
His body gleams amid eternal snows,
His tears fall from the skies.

I see his face in every flower;
The thunder and the singing of the birds
Are but his voice—and carven by his power
Rocks are his written words.

All pathways by his feet are worn,
His strong heart stirs the ever-beating sea,
His crown of thorns is twined with every thorn,
His cross is every tree.

Joseph Mary Plunkett

HOPE

He died!
And with him perished all that men hold dear;
Hope lay beside him in the sepulchre,
Love grew corse cold, and all things beautiful
    beside
Died when he died.

He rose!
And with him hope arose, and life and light.
Men said, "Not Christ but Death died yesternight."
And joy and truth and all things virtuous
    Rose when he rose.

Anonymous

GOOD FRIDAY

I for thy sake was pierced with heavy sorrow,
    And bore the cross,
Yet heeded not the sharpness of the arrow,
    Nor shame and loss.
Faint not, thou, whate'er thy burden be,
But bear it bravely, even to Calvary.

Girolamo Savonarola

From *OUR CHRIST*

I know not how that Calvary's cross
    A world from sin could free:
I only know its matchless love
    Has brought God's love to me.

I know not how that Joseph's tomb
    Could solve death's mystery:
I only know a living Christ,
    Our immortality.

Harry Webb Farrington

SIMON THE CYRENIAN SPEAKS

He never spoke a word to me,
    And yet he called my name,
He never gave a sign to me,
    And yet I knew and came.

At first I said, "I will not bear
    His cross upon my back;

He only seeks to place it there
        Because my skin is black."

But he was dying for a dream,
        And he was very weak,
And in his eyes there shone a gleam
        Men journey far to seek.

It was himself my pity bought;
        I did for Christ alone
What all of Rome could not have wrought
        With bruise of lash or stone.

                                        Countee Cullen

THE DISCIPLE

O friend, we never choose the better part
Until we set the cross up in the heart.
I know I cannot live until I die—
Till I am nailed upon it wild and high,
And sleep in the tomb for a full three days dead,
With angels at the feet and at the head.
But then in a great brightness I shall rise
To walk with stiller feet below the skies.

                                        Edwin Markham

THE CROSS UPON A HILL

The clouds of fear enshroud the earth,
        The tyrant hate is king:
All hearts are tense with memories
        Of Mars' wild trafficking.

The winter will not lose its hold
    Upon the hapless world.
The hopes of millions fail, with war's
    Red banners still unfurled.

And yet, against the darkened skies
    There stands a Cross of light;
Through centuries of human grief
    Its rays have pierced the night.
Still shall it stand, though despot rage
    Against the dreams of peace,
And it shall triumph in the end,
    And hate and strife shall cease.

The Cross of Christ—throughout the world
    Its rays shall ever shine.
For mankind, seized with fear and dread,
    That cross is God's own sign:
A sign of righteousness and truth,
    Of mercy and good will.
The hopes of men are in a Cross,
    A cross upon a hill.

                Thomas Curtis Clark

GOD'S WAY

I sought him in the still, far place where flowers blow
    In sun-bathed soil;
I found Him where the thousand life-streams flow
    Through sin and toil.

I listened for His step within the still, deep-cloistered shrine
    Of secret thought;
I heard it o'er the world's heart tumult, still divine,
    The Voice I sought.

I thought, far off, alone, to feel His presence by my side.
    His joy to gain;
I felt His touch upon life's weary pulse beside
    A bed of pain.

So those who seek the Master following their own way—
    Or gain, or loss—
Will find Him where their dreams of self are laid away,
    And there—a cross.

                    Dorothy Clarke Wilson

POEM

A candle is a lovely thing
    To light for Him tonight,
A slim white candle, straight and tall,
    To make the darkness bright.
But flickering out upon a Cross
    Upon a darkened hill,
It lit again—upon the Cross
    And it is burning still.

                    Anonymous

CRUCIFIXION

(On a Painting by Dali)
So witness once again the Crucified!
Upon this stretch of canvas now behold

This new unfoldment of a Christ who died.
And in two-point perspective, it is told,
This modern Crucifixion needs no nails—
Our age demands a sign less obsolete.
Yet mark the tide of hatred that prevails,
And in our world old agonies repeat.
Some ray of hope must light the darkened town
Where ancient suffering scarcely seems too strange.
And sure our day needs light . . . O Christ, look down!
Two thousand years have brought too little change.
The artist paints a hyper-cubic game:
The pain of Crucifixion is the same.

Mario Speracio

THE RED CROSS SPIRIT SPEAKS

Wherever war, with its red woes,
Or flood, or fire, or famine goes,
    There, too, go I;
If earth in any quarter quakes
Or pestilence its ravage makes,
    Thither I fly.

I go wherever men may dare,
I go wherever woman's care
    And love can live,
Wherever strength and skill can bring
Surcease to human suffering,
    Or solace give.

I helped upon Haldora's shore;
With Hospitaller Knights I bore
   The first red cross;
I was the Lady of the Lamp;
I saw in Solferino's camp
   The crimson loss.

I am your pennies and your pounds;
I am your bodies on their rounds
   Of pain afar;
I am you, doing what you would
If you were only where you could—
   Your avatar.

John H. Finley

A LITTLE PARABLE

I made the cross myself whose weight
   Was later laid on me.
This thought is torture as I toil
   Up life's steep Calvary.

To think mine own hands drove the nails!
   I sang a merry song,
And chose the heaviest wood I had
   To build it firm and strong.

If I had guessed—if I had dreamed
   Its weight was meant for me,
I should have made a lighter cross
   To bear up Calvary.

Anne Reeve Aldrich

HIGH ON A CROSS THEY NAILED HIM

High on a cross they nailed Him,
    And crowned Him with cruel thorns.
They pierced His side and mocked Him,
    Mocked Him with their scorns.

"Now," they cried, "The wicked one
    Can pursue his wicked way.
Jesus is gone, His life is done
    Unrighteousness can stay."

They put Him in an earthy tomb,
    Rejoicing in their mirth.
Forgetting that no flower can bloom
    'Til buried in the earth.

The rose that bloomed on Calvary,
    Two thousand years ago.
That rose shall bloom eternally
    To rid this world of woe.

                       Rhoda Newton

ALWAYS A CROSS

If any man would come after me, let him deny himself and take up his cross daily and follow me.—St. Luke 9:23

There is always a cross
    Where the Master has trod
But His cross brings no loss,
    But great glory to God.

                 Gilbert Darlington

THE CROSS

Talk not of Justice and her scales of woe,
We know no justice, weighing gain and loss,
Save the balancing arms of love held wide
That cannot sway or falter to and fro,
Mercy on this side and the other side,
The adamantine justice of the Cross.

Eva Gore-Booth

DISCIPLESHIP

O young and fearless prophet of ancient Galilee:
Thy life is still a summons to serve humanity,
To make our thoughts and actions less prone to please the
crowd,
To stand with humble courage for truth with hearts uncowed.

We marvel at the purpose that held Thee to Thy course,
While ever on the hilltop before Thee loomed the cross;
Thy steadfast face set forward where love and duty shone,
While we betray so quickly and leave Thee there alone.

O help us stand unswerving against war's bloody way,
Where hate and lust and falsehood hold back Christ's holy
sway;
Forbid the love of country, that blinds us to His call
Who lifts above the nation the brotherhood of all.

Create in us the splendor that dawns when hearts are kind,
That knows not race nor station as boundaries of the mind;
That learns to value beauty, in heart, or brain, or soul,
And longs to bind God's children into one perfect whole.

S. Ralph Harlow

❧❧ Sayings about the Cross

One is never so poignantly aware that another has lived, and of the whole meaning of that person's life, as in the moment of his death; and the manner of Jesus' death would have made this especially true in his case. Luke and, to a degree, Matthew, are interested in the date of Jesus' birth, and Luke provides a very elaborate dating of the beginning of his public ministry. But neither of these occurrences was remembered in the early church as the Crucifixion was—or rather, to say it better, Jesus himself was remembered in connection with his death as in connection with no other incident or phase of his career. This is the better way of saying it, for the reason that the memory we are considering was a memory of Jesus himself, not of any fact about him or any word he spoke. The memory of the death came very near to being the memory of the man. One could not remember Jesus without thinking of his cross, or remember the cross without thinking of him. The very act of the church in which its remembrance of Jesus was supremely expressed and continuously renewed was an act in which his body was broken and his blood poured out, a proclamation "of the Lord's death until he come." The Supper was "in remembrance of his death and passion," but only because it was, more profoundly, in remembrance of him.

John Knox,
The Early Church and the Coming Great Church

Five sayings from *The Passion of the King:*

Christ's cross is the "eternal" cross. His Passion is age-long. His dying is once for all, not merely during an hour (or three hours) of time, but an hour of eternity forced into time. And so we can go to him with our troubles, our sins, our miseries and frustrations. In fact, he bids us come: "I, when I am lifted up from the earth, will draw all men unto myself" (John 12:32). . . . For "my yoke is easy, and my burden is light" (Matt. 11:28–30). Easy? Light? when his yoke turned out to be a cross, so heavy that he himself stumbled and fell beneath the heavy timber (Mark 15:21). Yes: for the author of the *Imitation of Christ* said it truly: Christ's yoke is a cross, but it is a cross transformed, and transforming; its heaviness becomes lightness, and instead of being borne, it bears the one who carries it in the spirit of the Lord (compare 11.12, *De Regia via sanctae crucis*).

His death, in an even profounder sense than the poet's, was not failure but "transition": for it was to be merged in the victory of God's reign over the forces of evil, and would thus be transformed. It simply "would not count" as death, but only as victory.

Under the conditions which prevail in this present world

it may be necessary for a great many persons to endure a great amount of suffering—though they can still find inner joy and peace, a peace which the world can neither give nor take away.

The ordinary good person who goes quietly about his work refusing to be crushed and beaten by disasters—these persons exert a strength not their own.

The event of the cross (although it is incomplete without the Resurrection) marked the turning point in history, in all God's relations with the world, and the world's with God.

Frederick C. Grant

In the Bible three words express the darker and more difficult experiences of a religious life. They are: burden, thorn, cross. By "burden," both the Old and the New Testament mean the inevitable care and strain of earthly life. By "burden," we mean all our wearing daily tasks, duties which exhaust either by their monotony or their difficulty; the sleepless anxieties of our hearts that are a part of living; the sorrows of loneliness, poverty, disappointment, burdens of age, of sin. We can bear these burdens only as we cast them upon God and are sustained by his grace.

By "thorn" we mean the experience of a keener anguish—some weakness which makes us miserable. Paul spoke of his "thorn in the flesh" but never said what it was. Our thorn is our own private trouble, something which must be accepted, and endured by God-given strength to stand up under its hurt. Neither "burden" nor "thorn" can be escaped.

But often the individual "cross" can be escaped. It can be spurned or it can be taken up. Christ's cross for individuals varies. It is not the same for the same people all the time. What involved cross-bearing yesterday may become a joy today. If so, God would have us find a new and larger cross. The place where our own cross-bearing can best be measured is in our prayers. How much self-denial does their answering involve?

We do not need to fabricate crosses. We need simply to find those that are already here. We may wear a beautiful cross as a piece of religious symbolism, the external mark of our high regard for our Lord's dying. But is the cross of his discipleship in our heart?

J. Lane Miller

Six sayings from *His Cross and Ours*:

Even the Cross of Christ throws little light on the why of suffering; but it does show us how to suffer.

Suffering—deserved or undeserved—if voluntarily accepted, as a sacrament of the will of God, as Jesus accepted His Cross—a Cup from the hand of His Father, He called it— unveils the highest values of life, if indeed it does not create them. Anyway, it is the cost of priceless things in life, in faith, in art. Why this should be true nobody knows; but we know that it is true.

Three crosses, one hallowed by love, one hideous with hate, one pitiful with penitence; one man saved that none may despair, only one that none may dally or delay.

No one else saw the Cross as Mary saw it. To others Jesus was a Teacher, a Rebel, an Agitator, to His enemies an

Enemy, but to her He was a son, with all the tender memories and tugging meaning of motherhood.

No one of us may hope to know the full meaning of life or death, but at the Cross we can learn more of both than anywhere else.

It was not the Cross of Jesus, but His victory over the Cross, that set the world singing, and brought into the soul of man a new hope, a new joy, a new and haunting kind of goodness.

Joseph Fort Newton

Three sayings from *The Beginning of Christianity*:

Mark dates the crucifixion at nine o'clock in the morning. After Jesus had refused a narcotic drink, he was hung upon a cross and left to die of pain and exposure. The early tradition knew only one saying from the cross, the poignant words at the opening of the twenty-second Psalm, "My God, my God, why hast thou forsaken me?" It is blasphemous to speculate on the meaning of these words to Jesus, or on other thoughts which may have passed through his mind during the dark hours until death cut short his suffering. There is no possible interpreter of that agony. It is not to be contemplated with curiosity but with awe and wonder. But of one thing we can be certain: neither Mark nor any other early Christian could have looked upon the repetition of Scripture as a cry of despair. Jesus died with words of God upon his lips.

Christ was God's victor over the God-opposing powers. In the cross and resurrection, he had triumphed over the fallen angelic powers. Also, sin in the flesh had been condemned in Christ; his death did not mean the victory of sin, but was a triumph over it.

Simon of Cyrene was dropped entirely from the story of the crucifixion [in the Gospel of John]; John insisted that Jesus carried his own cross. He was not a phantom spirit but a creature of flesh and blood which could be handled and from whose side had flowed blood and water.

Clarence Tucker Craig

He [Christ] prayed on the cross. Of the seven "Words of the Cross" three and perhaps four are prayers. The prayer of pardon, "Father, forgive them, for they know not what they do," leaves us defenseless utterly.

George A. Buttrick, *Prayer*

Five sayings from *Meditations on the Gospel of St. John*:

If one were to try to construct a symbol representative of St. John's thinking, it would have to be something like a cross growing into a crown. It is not a case of carrying one's cross here in order that it may be exchanged for a crown else-where, but rather, of carrying a cross here which will, of itself, grow into a crown later.

In the body of the glorified Lord are still the dread marks of the cross. This must always color our attitude toward our own sufferings. These sufferings may be very great, or they may be very little, but, as crosses of our own, they are instru-ments of service both to God and to man. The patient endur-ance of affliction is truly noble, but it is still not enough. It must be evangelical in its concern. My pain increases my sensitivity to the pain of others, or I am wearing the cross, no matter how dreadful, as some form of personal decoration.

Christianity is the taking up of one's own cross and following Jesus. There are going to be wounds, but it is only by his wounds that his compassion is known.

I must learn out of my own knowledge, "I know that my Redeemer liveth." Christianity is nothing less than personal knowledge of the glorified and ascended Lord. . . . This is victory, this is triumph, this is life eternal, entered upon here and now.

[Referring to the *Respond* of Easter:] . . . glory moves from prose to poetry, from poetry to song, finally, to the only thing which I can reproduce—silence. When all the sounds are out of the way, and the distractions of beauteous trappings have merged in the middle distance, there he stands, he of the glorified wounds, my Lord and my God.

Canon Edward N. West

Christ was no less the Christ when he reached for the whip to drive the money-changers from the Temple; he was no less the Christ then, than when in that terrible hour of sacrifice he reached for the arms of a Cross.

Frederick Bruce Speakman

The key to the world is in the form of a cross. But it cannot do anything until someone's hand lifts it and fits it into the keyhole.

Howard C. Scharfe

I wish serenity and comfort to those who are especially loved by Jesus, since He has given them a share in His cross.
Pope Pius XII, Christmas Message, 1954

Five sayings and a prayer from *Meditations on the Cross*:

The Cross was not suicide. It was brought about by a strange providence through the social forces of the day.

It is not sufficient to meditate upon the Cross in its social and ethical aspects. It is only when we consider the religious aspect of the Cross that we get down to fundamentals.

It is hard for the Japanese people to grasp the Cross . . . there are few who really understand it, or fewer still who practice it. . . . The civilization of this present day is in exact opposition to the Cross, for it makes self the center, and puts its claim first.

The Cross is a way of conquering sorrow. Not suffering alone, but sorrow also is the lot of man. The teachings of Christianity make it possible to endure sorrow with a heart at peace.

The Cross is the conquest of death.

Father God: We thank Thee that we have been enabled to meditate on the Secret of Christ. As He chose the death of the Cross, fully embracing its ultimate bitterness, we, too, will walk the narrow path, chained to the Cross. Since this unworthy servant of Thine will henceforward move only as

bound on the Cross, I beseech Thee to lead even me in the
Way of Christ. Through Christ we pray. Amen.

Toyohito Kagawa,
tr. by Helen F. Topping and Marion R. Draper

Through this sign you shall conquer.

Constantine the Great, after his vision of
the cross following victory over Maxentius,
at Saxa Rubra, near Rome, October 27, 312

Two sayings from Thomas à Kempis, *The Imitation of Christ*:
In the cross there is safety.

Bk. II, chap. 12

If you rightly bear your cross, it will bear you.

Bk. II, chap. 5

God gives us the Cross, and the Cross gives us God.

Madame Guyon

It is three o'clock; the great Death has taken place, the
great Sacrifice is offered! The true Sin-offering for us, slain
without the camp. The true Burnt-offering, wholly dedicated,
wholly consumed upon the altar of the Cross—no part reserved in the greatness of His love. The true Peace-offering,
reconciling man to God in the sacramental stream which
ever flows from His pierced side.

Anthony Bathe, ed., *A Lent with Jesus*

Dominus regnavit a ligno. (The Lord is reigning from the
tree.)   Cf. Psalm 96:10

Traditional Eastern Orthodox Holy Thursday services were held yesterday, marking the approach of Easter in the calendar of Eastern Orthodox Churches (about thirteen days after the Easter of the Western Churches).

One of the first services here [New York City] was a celebration of the Divine Liturgy of St. Basil the Great at the Russian Orthodox Cathedral. A Holy Communion Service followed. The archbishop who is Metropolitan of the Russian Orthodox Church of North America presided. He then washed the feet of twelve priests, thus symbolizing Jesus' washing of the feet of the twelve Apostles the night of the first Lord's Supper.

The services of Easter will be introduced just before midnight tomorrow with processions around darkened churches and cathedrals. At midnight lights will flood the places of worship for Resurrection devotions. Lighted candles will be carried home by worshipers in the small hours of the morning, when the fast of Lent will be broken with feasting.

"The Easter of the Eastern Churches in New York,"
New York Times news story, April 17, 1955

In some respects Easter is the most beautiful of all the Christian observances. Its central concept, the dedication to the resurrection of Jesus, lies at the very core of the Christian faith and is its most sublime and triumphant achievement. This is the time at which men may rejoice in the victory of life over death, of light over darkness, of hope over despair.

It is no wonder, therefore, that this great festival has become adorned with so many symbols of beauty. They are the natural accompaniment of rejoicing, it is true, but their significance goes deeper. The flowers of Easter in themselves symbolize the resurrection of all natural life from the grim dark of winter. They are new-born in the never-ending miracle of resurrection. The music of Easter is that of a rich gladness, of a freshness of heart. However solemn may be its underlying themes, it finds its glory in a great embellishment, in the profound efflorescence of the truly beautiful that marks the Easter season.

The Easter season gains additional significance, moreover, from its historical coincidence with the great Jewish Festival of the Passover. This is the Feast of Deliverance, the celebration of the liberation from bondage and the tender mercy of the fatherly God. It links up inextricably with the Christian celebration of what is also a deliverance and what is likewise a hymn of praise to God's mercy and compassion.

> "On Easter Morning,"
> *New York Times* editorial, April 10, 1955

All glory be to thee, Almighty God, our heavenly Father, for that thou, of thy tender mercy, didst give thine only Son Jesus Christ to suffer death upon the Cross for our redemption; who made there (by his one oblation of himself once offered) a full, perfect, and sufficient sacrifice, oblation, and satisfaction, for the sins of the whole world; and did institute, and in his holy Gospel command us to continue, a perpetual memory of that his precious death and sacrifice, until his coming again.

> *From* The Prayer of Consecration, in The Order
> for Administration of the Lord's Supper, *The*
> *Book of Common Prayer*

Collects concerning the cross, from
The Book of Common Prayer:

Almighty God, whose most dear Son went not up to joy
but first he suffered pain, and entered not into the glory
before he was crucified; Mercifully grant that we, walking in
the way of the cross, may find it none other than the way of
life and peace; through the same thy Son Jesus Christ our
Lord. *Amen.*

Monday before Easter

Almighty Father, whose dear Son, on the night before he
suffered, did institute the Sacrament of his Body and Blood;
Mercifully grant that we may thankfully receive the same in
remembrance of him, who in these holy mysteries giveth us a
pledge of life eternal; the same thy Son Jesus Christ our
Lord, who now liveth and reigneth with thee and the Holy
Spirit ever, one God, world without end. *Amen.*

Thursday before Easter,
commonly called Maundy Thursday

Almighty God, we beseech thee graciously to behold this
thy family, for which our Lord Jesus Christ was contented to
be betrayed, and given up into the hands of wicked men, and
to suffer death upon the cross; who now liveth and reigneth
with thee and the Holy Ghost ever, one God, world without
end. *Amen.*

Good Friday

Grant, O Lord, that as we are baptized into the death of
thy blessed Son, our Saviour Jesus Christ, so by continual

mortifying our corrupt affections we may be buried with him; and that through the grave, and gate of death, we may pass to our joyful resurrection; for his merits, who died, and was buried, and rose again for us, the same thy Son Jesus Christ our Lord. *Amen.*

Easter Even

O God, who for our redemption didst give thine only-begotten Son to the death of the Cross, and by his glorious resurrection hast delivered us from the power of our enemy; Grant us so to die daily from sin, that we may evermore live with him in the joy of his resurrection; through the same thy Son Christ our Lord. *Amen.*

Easter Day

I believe in God the Father Almighty, Maker of heaven and earth: and in Jesus Christ his only Son our Lord: Who was conceived by the Holy Ghost, Born of the Virgin Mary: Suffered under Pontius Pilate, Was crucified, dead, and buried: He descended into hell; The third day he rose again from the dead.

from The Apostles' Creed

✿ Glossary of Terms and Religious Symbols in Art and Liturgy

ACORN: immortality; strength.

AGNUS DEI: Lamb of God; ancient symbol for Jesus.

ALMOND: divine favor; hope.

ALPHA: Greek letter for "A," denoting "beginning."

ALTAR: elevated area on which offerings were placed in ancient times, and where sacred rites were observed. In churches, focal point of edifice; Communion table. Symbol of worship.

AMPULLA: glass or metal vessel for consecrated oil; occasionally used instead of word "cruet."

ANCHOR: hope; concealed cross, in Early Christian art.

ANGEL: messenger of God.

ANKH: *crux ansata*, Egyptian T-shaped cross with handle; key of life.

ANT: industriousness.

ANTEPENDIA: cloth or metal covering of altar, lectern, etc. of church.

APSE: semicircular, polygonal, or rectangular extension of altar end of church.

ARK: salvation; Church; eternity.

ARROW: instrument of martyrdom.

ASHES: penitence; grief.

ASS: patience; humility.

AUREOLE: elongated formation of light rays around depiction of sacred subject.

AX (BATTLE): instrument of martyrdom.

BANNER: victory.

BARBÉE: fish-hooked ends of square cross.

BEE: resurrection; chaste life; zealous activity.

BELL: summons to worship.

BIRDS: souls of the righteous.

BOAT: *see* Ship.

BOAT HOOK: if used with saltire: St. Andrew; if used with fish: St. Simon; if used with builder's square: St. Jude.

BOOK: Bible, or specific parts of it, or religious writings (as of Great Fathers).

BREAD: spiritual life; in loaves, marked with crosses, the Eucharist.

BREASTPLATE: righteousness; priestly calling; Aaron; the Old Testament.

BUDDING ROD: Aaron; Joseph of Nazareth; of Arimathaea.

BULL: strength; sacrifice; St. Ambrose.

BULRUSHES WITH BASKET: Moses as a child.

BUSH, BURNING: Moses' call.

BUTTERFLY: the Resurrection.

CAMEL: temperance.

CAMPANILE: free-standing bell tower.

CANDLE: Jesus as Light of World; worship.

CANDLESTICK: *two-branched*: dual nature of Christ; *three-branched*: Trinity; *five-branched*: wounds of Jesus; *seven-branched* (Jewish Menorah): perfect number.

CENSER: burner for incense; symbol of worship.

CHALICE: cup or goblet used in celebration of the Eucharist (Holy Communion, Mass, Lord's Supper, Holy Mysteries, Divine Liturgy); symbol of the Eucharist or Faith.

CHANCEL: portion of church east (liturgically) of the crossing.

CHASUBLE: poncholike outer vestment worn by Celebrant (except Eastern bishops) at Eucharist; symbol of character.

CHERUBIM: celestial beings, four-winged and "full of eyes," symbolic of God's nearness.

CHOIR: space separated from rest of church or cathedral anciently reserved exclusively for the clergy. In Gothic cathedrals, the choir is between the apse and the principal crossing.

CIBORIUM: metal vessel for holding breads or the Reserved Communion elements; anciently, an arched canopy over an altar.

CIRCLE: endless life, immortality; perfection; as in Celtic crosses.

CLERESTORY: portion of ecclesiastical building which rises above roofs of aisles or transepts, allowing access to light.

CLOISTER: covered walk along one or more sides of an enclosed space, with center open to sky; often serving as place of meditation.

COCK: denial of Christ by St. Peter; vigilance.

COLONNADE: series of columns joined by an entablature.

COLORS, LITURGICAL: the following material is from an article written by Canon Edward N. West and published by Whittemore Associates, Inc.:

The earliest definite knowledge of the use of specific

colour in the service of the Church is Clement of Alexandria's recommendation of white as suitable to all Christians. The Canons of Hippolytus assign white to the clergy as becoming their office. The mediaeval development of colour symbolism may be examined in the Rationale Divinorum Officiorum of Durandus. This 13th Century prelate explains the meanings of all colours but, interestingly enough, knows of no such thing as either a standard Use or a standard meaning.

The ancient Use of liturgical colours was relatively simple; the best, the second best, ordinary, and, in some places, black. The Eastern Orthodox Church still adheres to this practice. In so far as "the best" is concerned, it is still required by the Dominican Order's Rule to be worn on the highest feasts irrespective of its colour.

In the middle ages each Cathedral had its own Use, and although this Use was in no sense binding on the Diocese involved, it was inevitable that some sequences should become popular and that, ultimately, certain Cathedral Uses should grow wider even than diocesan in their influence. It must be remembered, however, that on an Ascension Day in the 16th Century, one could still have seen "the best" vestments used in Salisbury; white, in Westminster; blue, in the College of St. Bernard at Romans; yellow, in Prague; red, in Utrecht; and green, in Soissons.

The Use of Salisbury Cathedral (Sarum) has always had wide popularity, therefore, it is listed here—but it should be noted that the ancient Westminster Use, which was predominately white, red, and black, has always had considerable appeal to northern taste.

The best: Christmas, Epiphany, Easter, Ascension, Whitsunday, Trinity, Dedication, Patronal Festival, All Saints', Thanksgiving.

Second best: Weekdays in Epiphanytide, Trinitytide (if red be not used).

RED: In Octave of Epiphany, Sundays after Epiphany, Septuagesima to Ash Wednesday, Passiontide to Easter Eve, Sundays after Trinity, Holy Innocents; Martyrs, Apostles and Evangelists (except St. John).

WHITE: St. John the Evangelist, during Octave of Christmas, Circumcision, Eastertide, Rogation Days, Friday and Saturday before Whitsunday, during Octave of Trinity, Feasts of the B.V.M., Saints' days in Eastertide, Virgins, Michaelmas.

BLUE: Advent, and as alternative colour for Pre-Lenten Season, Nativity of St. John Baptist, All Souls' Day, Funerals and Requiems.

BLACK: All Souls' Day, Funerals and Requiems.

UNBLEACHED LINEN: Days of Lent until Passion Sunday.

The Colour Sequence of the Roman Catholic Church is now very largely that common to the Court of Rome in the 16th Century. It is often referred to as the Western Use. It is as follows:

WHITE: Christmas and days of Octave; Circumcision, Epiphany and Octave; Maundy Thursday; Easter Even through the 5th Sunday after Easter; Ascension Eve through to Vigil of Pentecost; Trinity Sunday; Corpus Christi and Octave; Transfiguration; Christ the King; Feasts of the B.V.M.; All Saints' and Octave; Michaelmas; Confessors, Doctors, Virgins, and Holy Women.

RED: Pentecost and Octave; Apostles and Evangelists (except St. John whose feast is a white one); Martyrs; (the Holy Innocents, only if that feast falls on a Sunday).

VIOLET: Advent Season—except the third Sunday, "Gaudete"; Septuagesima through to Maundy Thursday—except the Fourth Sunday, "Laetare"; Ember Days apart from the Octave of Pentecost; Rogation Days; Vigils; Holy Innocents, if not on a Sunday.

GREEN: The Sundays (and Ferias) after the Octave of the Epiphany through to the Eve of Septuagesima; the Sundays (and Ferias) after Pentecost (or, after Trinity) through to Advent.

BLACK: Good Friday; All Souls'; Requiems.

ROSE: The Third Sunday in Advent; the Fourth Sunday in Lent.

The Lutheran rules on Paraments are strict and clear: the Altar vestments, hangings, Pulpit and Lectern falls, et cetera, are invariably of the Day or the Season irrespective of the Service involved. The colour Use is:

WHITE: Christmas Eve through Epiphanytide; Easter Day to Whitsun Eve; Feasts: Transfiguration, Presentation, Trinity Sunday through Octave, Annunciation, Visitation, and Michaelmas.

RED: First Vespers of Whitsunday to First Vespers of Trinity Sunday; Festival of the Reformation (October 31) and the Sunday nearer it; Feasts: Apostles (except St. John), Martyrs, All Saints; Dedication of a Church, Church Anniversaries, Harvest Festival, and Thanksgiving Day.

GREEN: First Vespers of Septuagesima through Shrove Tuesday, II Trinity through to the First Vespers of I Advent.

VIOLET: First Vespers of I Advent to Christmas Eve, Vespers of Shrove Tuesday through to Vespers of Easter Even (excepting Good Friday).

BLACK: Good Friday, and for a Day of Humiliation.

The Fair Linen is required to be long enough to reach from one third to two thirds the distance from the top of the Altar to the floor, and wide enough to hang over the front (and back) a full span.

COLORS, SYMBOLIC: *black*: penitence; *blue*: heavenly truth, sanctification; *gold*: worth, virtue, glory of God; *green*: eternal youth, hope; *purple*: dignity; *purple-blue*: tranquillity; *purple-red*: severity; *red*: divine zeal, creative fire, love of God; *violet*: humility, suffering, mourning, sympathy; *yellow* (*bright*): truthfulness, beneficence; *yellow* (*dull*): deceitfulness.

CORNUCOPIA: plenty; Thanksgiving; Asher.

CREDENCE: small shelf or table on which are placed the necessary elements for Communion service.

CROCODILE: hypocrisy.

CROCUS: joy.

CROOK: Abel; Moses; David; Amos; chief pastor, as bishop; or abbot.

CROSIER: originally, the cross-staff of a bishop; now used loosely to describe a shepherd's crook or pastoral staff.

CROSS (300 or more forms in existence—*see* this book, *A Treasury of the Cross, passim*): Redemption; the Faith.

CROSSING: space in cruciform church where transept and nave intersect.

CROWN: spiritual rank (as martyrs); earthly dignity (as David, or Kings of the East).

CRUCIFIX: figure of Christ on cross: if naked: the Suffering Saviour; if clothed: the Reigning Victorious Christ.

CYPRESS: eternal life; sorrow.

DECUSSATA (CRUX): X-shaped cross, or saltire, symbolizing St. Andrew.

DOG: loyalty.

DOOR: Christ (as in John 10:9); if jambs are sprinkled with blood: the Passover.

DOSSAL *or* DORSAL: decorative textile, hanging back of altar.

DOVE: the Holy Spirit; purity; peace; many kindred meanings if used in combination with other symbols.

EAGLE: Christ; the Gospel; St. John the Evangelist.

ECCLESIOLOGIST: specialist in ecclesiastical architecture and symbolism.

ENCOLPION: pectoral image worn by a Greek bishop; formerly, it was invariably a reliquary. Same as "Panagia."

EPIPHANY: Christian term applied to January 6 festival honoring Christ's manifestation in the Western Church, to Gentiles through visit of Wise Men (Magi); in the Eastern Church, through his Baptism.

EWER: flagon of water to be used in Baptism.

EYE, WIDE OPEN: the all-seeing God; enclosed in triangle: God the Father.

FAÏENCE: fine-quality glazed earthenware, generally highly colored; used in making accessories for altars, plaques, etc.

FAIR LINEN CLOTH: cover for top of the altar, usually having five crosses embroidered, one at each corner of the top of the altar, and one in center, signifying the wounds of Jesus. It hangs almost to the floor at the sides, and several inches over front of the altar. Many churches are now restoring the use of linen all the way to the floor on all four sides. Symbolizes linen worn at Christ's burial.

FITCHÉE: pointed lower end of cross, enabling it, in theory, to be driven upright into the ground.

FLAGON: covered container used to hold wine for Communion.

FLAMES, TONGUES OF: Pentecost.

FLEUR-DE-LIS: device used in symbolic art, resembling three petals of iris held together by band, denoting Trinity or the Blessed Virgin Mary.

FLEURY: flower-petaled terminals of arms of crosses.

FOOT: humility.

FONT: receptacle in which, or over which, Baptism is performed.

FRESCO: technically, painting made by applying colors to wall or ceiling before plaster is dry, so that pigments fuse; in general, any form of wall painting.

FRONTAL: removable hanging or cover for front (and sides, or all four sides) of altar.

FRONTLET: among the Hebrews, phylactery or small case worn on head and containing slip inscribed Deut. 6:8, 11:18, to remind wearer to keep Law.

FURCHÉE: form of cross having four forked arms.

FYLFOT: hooked cross with shorter "gamma" arms than a swastika; arms turning clockwise.

GARGOYLE: medieval type of waterspout terminating in grotesque head or figure; symbol of evil passions driven away by Gospel.

GATE: entrance to heaven; the Blessed Virgin.

GOSPEL SIDE: left side of altar as congregation faces it.

GRADINE: shelf above and behind altar, but, technically, not attached to.

GRAPES: union of Christ's followers with him; the Eucharist.

HAND (*manus Dei*): chief symbol of God the Father. In Latin art, the thumb and first two fingers are extended; in Greek art, the forefinger is extended upward, the second and little fingers bent in a semicircle, with the thumb crossing the completely closed-down third finger.

HARP: heaven's music; praise through joyful worship; David; St. Cecilia.

HART: soul of the faithful, painting for God (Ps. 42:1).

HEART: Christian love (charity); if pierced with sword: Blessed Virgin; if pierced with two arrows: St. Augustine of Hippo.

HORN: God's bounty; horn of oil: David.

HORSE: and rider: Christ; with white banner: St. James Major.

HOUSE ON ROCK: Christian faith established on Christ.

HYSSOP: Christ's passion; absolution.

ICHTHUS: Greek word for "fish," which as acrostic spells "Jesus Christ, God's Son, Saviour." The fish itself is used thus in early catacombs art and elsewhere.

ICON: from Greek *eikón* meaning a likeness, as represented in painting, enamel, mosaic, metal, etc. to depict a sacred personage or event.

ICONOCLAST: one who by action or word mars or destroys images or traditional beliefs.

ICONOGRAPHY: expression in art of idea, person, or event; analysis of materials used in symbolic art.

ICONOLATRY: worship of icons, in terms forbidden by the Church.

ICONOLOGY: knowledge dealing with representational art.

ICONOSCOPE: in television, cathode-ray tube that focuses image scanned by cathode-ray beam.

ICONOSTASIS: in Eastern Orthodox Church: a screen or partition upon which the specifically required icons are placed; it separates main part of church from sanctuary.

INCENSE: worship.

INCISE: to engrave, as for inscriptions and decorations.

INTAGLIO: design or figure cut below surface, as in gems or seals carrying symbols.

IVY: constancy; memory.

KEY or MEANDER PATTERN: no beginning and no ending; eternity.

KEYS: St. Peter.

LABARUM: Roman military standard; especially, in Christian art, labarum of Constantine the Great which carried symbol of victorious Christ.

LADDER: accessory of the Crucifixion; Jacob.

LAMB: purity; innocence; St. John the Baptist.

LAMB CARRYING BANNER: *Ecce Angus Dei* ("Behold, the Lamb of God").

LAMP: worship; knowledge.

LANCE: instrument of martyrdom; Passion symbol; with three stones: St. Matthias; with carpenter's square: St. Thomas; with fuller's bat: St. Jude.

LAUREL: victor's truimph.

LAVABO: metal or glass bowl or basin for ceremonial washing of hands.

LECTERN: reading desk, now generally used for Scripture.

LENT: from Anglo-Saxon description of start of lengthening days of spring; it now indicates the season when Christians prepare to participate in the Paschal Mystery at Easter.

In the West it begins with Ash Wednesday and includes forty weekdays before Easter; in the East, it lasts forty-eight days: the Great Fast of Forty Days plus the Fast of Christ's Passions.

LILY: the Annunciation; purity; heavenly joy.

LION: courageous strength; royalty (Jesus, "the Lion of the tribe of Judah").

LITANY DESK: a kneeler placed in the body of the center aisle of church, where special supplications are offered.

LITURGY: collection of forms of public worship, more especially the Eucharist.

LIZARD: transfiguring power of Gospel.

LOTUS (in Far East): heart of man; purity.

LUNETTE: arched space in long vault; crescent-shaped decorative panel.

LYRE: sacred music.

MANGER: Christ's nativity.

MANUS DEI (hand of God): *see* Hand.

MARIGOLD: the Blessed Virgin.

MENORAH: seven-branched candlestick—a central stem with three branches on each side—in Tabernacle of Hebrews and still used in synagogues.

MENSA: top surface of altar, actually the table part.

MITRE: headdress worn by bishops and other ecclesiastical leaders. The Old Testament mitre is shown divided from front to back; Western Christian mitres are divided from side to side; Eastern Orthodox mitres are in reality crowns and have no divisions.

MOLINE: form of cross whose terminals resemble the moline (iron on lower side of millstone); an alternative form of anchor cross.

MONEY (coins): thirty pieces: Judas' betrayal.

MONEY BAG: St. Cyril; three bags: St. Matthew.

MONOGRAMS: characters containing two or more letters, to
indicate words of sacred significance:

X P earliest known, the *Chrismon* or Chi Rho used on
labarum of Constantine the Great and signifying first
two letters of word Christ, in Greek.

A Ω Alpha and Omega, Christ the beginning, Christ the
end, the all-in-all.

IC XC Jesus Christ. The first and last letters of Jesus and
of Christ in Greek.

IHS *or* IHC: familiar monogram for "Jesus," consisting of
first three letters or first two and last, of the name Jesus
in Greek. The late Latin interpretation, *Iesus Homino-
rum Salvator* ("Jesus, the Saviour of Men"), is deplored
by all scholars.

IHC: more ancient form of IHS.

INBI: abbreviation of Greek inscription above cross:
IHCOYC o NAZΩPAIOS o BACIΛEYC TΩN
IOYΔAIΩN, and

INRI: abbreviation of Latin inscription: *Iesus Nazarenus
Rex Iudaeorum. Both* INBI and INRI mean "Jesus of
Nazareth, the King of the Jews."

MONSTRANCE: pyx or vessel in which the Reserved Host of
the Eucharist is displayed.

MOON: the Virgin Mary; when used with sun at Crucifixion: the horror of all creation at the Passion of Christ.

MOSAIC: medium often employed for depicting sacred art
and symbols, by means of tiny cubes (tesserae) of glass,
marble, or semiprecious stones cut so as to reflect maxi-

mum light, or covered with glass or gold, and set in background of cement or plaster.

MYRRH: the priestly office of Christ; with aloes, in container: Passion of Jesus; purity.

MYRTLE: physical purity.

NAILS, THREE: Passion of Christ.

NARTHEX: space at rear of church and separate from it, used in ancient days for catechumens and penitents.

NAVE: from Latin *navis* meaning ship; main portion of church, from narthex or vestibule to chancel.

NIKA: Greek word for "victor" often embodied in symbol by placing in four corners of Greek cross, IC (Jesus), XC (Christ), and NI KA (Victor). (See drawing p. 60.) Used by Greek Church on Eucharistic bread.

NIMBUS: Latin for "cloud-shaped splendour"; stylized disk behind head of divine or sacred personage. May be circular, rectangular, triangular, hexagonal.

OAK: eternity; strength. Occasionally, design on fonts.

OLIVE: peace; healing; Noah; in gnarled tree: Gethsemane; the Archangel Gabriel.

OMER: Hebrew measuring unit; symbolic of manna.

ORANS *or* ORANTE: praying human figure, arms extended, symbol of prayer, or martyr, or individual soul.

PALL: linen cover for chalice; cloth cover for coffin; bishop's or archbishop's pallium (Y-shaped scarf placed on shoulders).

PALM: victory; spiritual triumph; martyrdom; the Archangel Gabriel.

PALLIUM: *see* Pall.

PANAGIA: *see* Encolpion.

PANTOCRATOR: almighty, omnipotent, used to describe certain icons of Christ.

PARAMENTS: frontals and hangings for altars, lectern, and pulpits, colors varying for different seasons of church year; *see* Color.

PASCHAL CANDLE: single large candle lighted on Easter Even and used continually until Ascension Day.

PATEN: precious metal plate for bread or wafers to be consecrated at Eucharist.

PATTÉE *or* PATY: cross having the arms curved outward, with straight ends.

PEACOCK: immortality.

PECTORAL: cross or reliquary box, worn on breast; a pectoral cross is one of the ornaments of a bishop in Western Christianity.

PELICAN: Atonement.

PHOENIX: Resurrection.

PILGRIM'S HAT AND STAFF: St. James Major.

POMEGRANATE BURSTING WITH SEEDS: Resurrection; immortality; decoration on ancient Hebrew priestly garments.

PREDELLA: step immediately beneath altar.

PRIE-DIEU: low prayer desk with kneeler attached.

PROCESSIONAL CROSS: one designed to be carried on end of staff.

PULPIT: Word of God.

PYRAMID: with star: flight into Egypt.

QUATREFOIL: four-petaled symbol in ecclesiastical decorations.

RAINBOW: God's promise to Noah; Lord's seat at the Last Judgment.

RAM: sacrifice: Isaac's sacrifice.

RELIQUARY: case or amulet of metal, wood, etc., intended to hold sacred relic.

REPOUSSÉE: relief made by hammering design on reverse side of metal.

REREDOS: screen behind altar, of wood, textile, stone, marble, painting, mosaics.

RETABLE *or* GRADINE: low shelf standing behind and above altar on which reredos rests.

RIVERS, FOUR, OF PARADISE: Four Gospels; the Four Evangelists.

ROCK: stable character; Christ.

ROOD: large crucifix placed on screen which separates nave of church from chancel or choir; man's journey from Church Militant to Church Triumphant.

ROSARY: in the Eastern Church: a string of beads used as an aid in saying the Jesus Prayer; in the Western Church: a string of 15 large and 150 small beads (possibly originating with St. Dominic) for counting group of prayers—fifteen decades of the Hail, Mary, each preceded by the Lord's Prayer and followed by the *Gloria Patri.*

ROSE: Christ; Nativity; the Virgin Mary (especially white rose); red rose: martyrdom; on cross: Christ's death. A conventionalized five-petaled rose is called the Tudor or Gothic rose.

SACKCLOTH AND ASHES: penitence; mourning.

SACRISTY: room where ecclesiastical vestments, Communion vessels, and treasures are kept.

SALTIRE: X shaped; e.g., two crossed keys in saltire: St. Andrew.

SANCTUARY: area immediately surrounding altar.

SCALES (BALANCES): justice; with flaming sword: the Archangel Michael.

SCEPTER: kingly authority.

SCREEN: as, rood screen of carved stone or wood.

SCROLL: Scriptures; individual writings of saints (as with word *Theotokos*, St. Cyril).

SERPENT: evil; Satan; wisdom.

SHAMROCK: the Trinity; St. Patrick.

SHEAF OF GRAIN: God's bounty; Joseph's dream.

SHEEP AND GOATS: the saved and the lost.

SHELL (especially escallop): pilgrimage; Baptism; St. James Major.

SHEPHERD, WITH LAMB ACROSS SHOULDERS: early Christian symbol indicating nature of Christ.

SHIELD: safety; protection.

SHIP: St. Simon; Christ's Church; emblem of The World Council of Churches.

SKULL: transitoriness of life on earth; Adam.

SQUIRREL: spiritual pondering.

STAG: Christ; two stags drinking: Baptism.

STAR: *five-pointed*: Bethlehem, Jesse, Epiphany; *six-pointed*: God the Father, star of David; *seven-pointed*: gifts of Holy Spirit; *eight-pointed*: regeneration; *nine-pointed*: fruits of the Spirit; *ten-pointed*: the faithful disciples; *twelve-pointed*: Twelve Disciples.

STELE: upright stone or slab of stone, etc., carrying significant inscription—often religious.

STOLE: narrow textile scarf worn over shoulders of clergy, originally a towel.

STONE: instrument of martyrdom; hardness of heart; deacon's dalmatic and three stones: St. Stephen; three stones: St. James the Less.

SUN: God the Father; if circling IHC: Jesus, Sun of Righteousness.

SUNFLOWER: Christian turning toward Christ.

SUPPEDANEUM: footrest on cross.

SURPLICE: white linen garment worn over cassock.

SWORD: instrument of martyrdom; with open Bible displaying words *Spiritus gladius* ("Sword of the Spirit"): St. Paul.

TABLETS, TWO: Ten Commandments.

TEMPERA: method of painting, especially murals, in which paint is mixed with binder, such as egg blended with water.

TENT: Israel in Wilderness.

TESSERA: small cube of stone or glass, unit of mosaic art, when laid in plaster or cement, after being cut in fashion to reflect maximum radiance.

THORNS, CROWN OF: Passion of Christ.

TRACERY: ornamental stonework filling in upper areas of Gothic windows or panels.

TRANSEPT: arm of cruciform church at right angles to nave.

TREES: *acacia*: immortality; *banana* (S. India): life; *cedar*: growth, integrity; *evergreen*: eternal life; *fig*: fruitfulness, fidelity; *mustard:* growth from small start; *oak:* strength; *olive*: healing, faith, beauty; *olive branch* (dove): deliverance from hardship; *palm*: triumphant entry into Jerusalem, victory.

TREFOIL: Trinity.

TRIANGLE, EQUILATERAL: Trinity.

TRIBES, THE TWELVE, EMBLEMS OF: *Judah*: lion; *Ephraim*:

vine; *Issachar*: ass; *Benjamin*: wolf; *Zebulun*: ship; *Manasseh*: palm; *Reuben*: sea; *Dan*: serpent; *Simeon*: sword; *Asher*: vase; *Gad*: banner; *Naphthali*: hind.

TRIPTYCH: three-leaved carving or painting, generally used behind altar.

TRUMPET: call to worship; Resurrection; Judgment Day.

TURTLE DOVE: constancy; the Presentation.

TYMPANUM: arched space over doorway.

TWELVE: Apostles; various symbols not mentioned elsewhere in Glossary are: St. Peter: inverted Latin cross; St. John the Evangelist: chalice with serpent rising; St. James the Less: saw; St. Philip: two loaves; St. Bartholomew: flaying knives on Bible; St. Simon Zelotes: fish on book; Judas: blank shield.

VEIL: covering for chalice; as symbol, religious life.

VESTMENTS: ecclesiastical apparel for clergy; covering for altar.

VESICA: symbol of conventionalized fish (*ichthus*) formed by two intersecting segments of a circle.

VINE: fellowship of Christ and believers; the Eucharist.

WALLET: pilgrim's journey.

WATER LILY: charity.

WELL: refreshing of spirit; living Water.

WHEAT IN SHEAF: God's bounty; with tares: the Church; with grapes: the Eucharist.

WHEEL: winged: Holy Spirit, the Cherubim; with knives: St. Catherine.

WILLOW: death; sorrow.

WINGS: aspiring soul; indication of supernatural being.

YOKE: long-suffering patience; burden-bearing; the Law.

✂ Bibliography

Baldwin, Marshall W., *The Mediaeval Church*, Cornell University Press, Ithaca, N.Y., 1953.

Bridgeman, Charles T., *The Ancient Churches of the Near East*, The Near East Society, New York (Monograph Series 15, 1951, 1952).

Christian Sects of the Near East. The Near East Society, New York (Monograph Series 6, 1948).

Cullman, Oscar, *Early Christian Worship*, Henry Regnery Company, Chicago, Ill., 1953.

Fernand Cabrol *et* Henri Leclerque, eds., *Dictionnaire d'Archéologie Chrétienne et de Liturgie*, Vol. 3, Pt. 2, Librairie Letouzey et Ané, Paris, 1934 ff.

Dumbarton Oaks Research Library and Collection, Bulletin Number One, Dumbarton Oaks Research Library, Washington, D.C., 1950.

Fleming, Daniel Johnson, *Christian Symbols in a World Community*, The Friendship Press, New York, 1940.

Gardner, Helen, *Art through the Ages*, Harcourt, Brace, and Company, New York, 1936.

Grant, Frederick C., *The Passion of the King*, The Macmillan Company, New York, 1955.

Griffith, Helen Stuart, *The Sign Language of Our Faith*, Morehouse-Gorham Co., New York, 1954.

Guide to Early Christian and Byzantine Antiquities of the Department of British and Mediaeval Antiquities of the British

Museum, Trustees of the British Museum, London, 1921.

Koch, Rudolph, *The Book of Signs,* The First Editions Club, London, 1930.

Kraeling, Karl H., "Christian Burial Urns," article in *The Biblical Archaeologist,* February, 1946, IX, 1.

Meyer, Peter, *Introduction to Byzantine Mosaics—Torcello, Venice, Monreale, Palermo, Cefalu,* Oxford University Press, New York, Toronto, 1952.

Metropolitan Museum Studies, Vol. III, Pt. 2, The Metropolitan Museum of Art, New York, 1931.

Miller, Madeleine S. and J. Lane, *Harper's Bible Dictionary,* art. Crosses, Symbols, and *passim,* Harper & Brothers, New York, 1952, 1954, 1955, 1956.

Morey, Charles Rufus, *Early Christian Art,* Princeton University Press, Princeton, N.J., 1942.

Morrison, James Dalton, ed., *Masterpieces of Religious Verse,* Harper & Brothers, New York, 1948.

Newton, Joseph Fort, *His Cross and Ours,* Harper & Brothers, New York, 1941.

Prentice, Sartell, *The Voices of the Cathedral,* William Morrow and Company, New York, 1938.

Rest, Friedrich, *Our Christian Symbols,* The Christian Education Press, Philadelphia, Pa., 1954.

Schweinfurth, Philipp, *Russian Icons,* Oxford University Press, London, 1953.

Seymour, William Wood, *The Cross in Tradition, History and Art,* G. P. Putnam's Sons, The Knickerbocker Press, New York, 1898.

Smith, Earl Baldwin, *Early Christian Iconography,* Princeton University Press, Princeton, N.J., 1918.

Smith, H. J., *Symbols and Emblems,* T. S. Leach & Company, Philadelphia, Pa., 1900.

Stafford, Thomas A., *Christian Symbolism in the Evangelical Churcl.es,* Abingdon Press, Nashville, 1942.

Twining, Louisa, *Symbols and Emblems of Early and Mediaeval Christianity,* John Murray, London, 1885.

Webber, Frederick Roth, *Church Symbolism*, J. H. Jansen, Cleveland, Ohio, 1938.

Wells, George Ferguson, *A Book of Symbols*, Oxford University Press, New York, 1954.

West, Edward N., *Meditations on the Gospel of St. John*, Harper & Brothers, New York, 1955.

Woodruff, Helen, and Morey, Charles Rufus, *The Index of Christian Art at Princeton University* (pamphlet), Princeton University Press, Princeton, N.J., 1942.

Young, George, *Constantinople*, Methuen & Co., Ltd., London, 1926.

Index